A CALL TO LOVE

Chiara Lubich

A CALL TO LOVE
Spiritual Writings, Volume 1

New City Press

Published in the United States by New City Press
206 Skillman Avenue, Brooklyn, New York, 11211
©1989 New City Press, New York

Translated by Hugh Moran from the original Italian
Il Si dell'Uomo a Dio (©1980)
La Parola di Vita (©1974)
L'Eucaristia (©1977)
©Città Nuova Editrice, Rome, Italy

Cover design by Nick Cianfarani

Library of Congress Cataloging-in-Publication Data:

Lubich Chiara, 1920–
  A call to love.

  (Spiritual writings ; v. 1)
  Translated from the Italian.
  Contents: Our yes to God — The word of life — The Eucharist.
  1. God — Will. 2. Christian Life — Catholic authors. 3. Lord's Supper —
Catholic Church. 4. Catholic Church — Doctrines. 5. Focolare Movement.
I. Title. II. Series: Lubich, Chiara, 1920–   . Prose works.
English. Selections ; v. 1.
  BX2350.2.L7762513 vol. 1   248.4'82 s   89-8320
  ISBN 0-911782-67-2   [248.4'82]

Scripture quotations in *Our Yes to God* are from the Revised Standard Version,
©1973. Special permission granted to use "in this publication" the you-your-
yours form of the personal pronoun in the address of God. Quotations marked
with an asterisk are from the New American Bible, ©1970, Confraternity of
Christian Doctrine.
Scripture quotations in *The Word of Life* and *The Eucharist* are from the New
American Bible.

Printed in the United States of America

CONTENTS

FOREWORD

Chiara Lubich is a prominent figure in ecumenism and in the growing dialogue between the world's great religions. Her own experience of life coincides with the founding and development of the Focolare movement extended throughout the world and whose spiritual basis and inspiration lies principally in the prayer of Jesus, "may they all be one" (Jn 17:21).

In 1987, Chiara was appointed by Pope John Paul II an observer to the Synod of Bishops on the Vocation and Mission of the Laity. In this occasion she delivered an address outlining the spiritualities of the numerous ecclesial movements that have lately risen within the Church.

Since publishing in 1959 her first book entitled *Meditations,* Chiara has written extensively on a variety of spiritual topics drawn from the gospel message and in a particular way seen from the angle of unity. Since the list of her works continually increases, we thought it now useful to composite them into volumes of which this is the first to appear. It binds together three of her previous works which develop some of the specific points brought to light in her address at the Synod.

The first, *Our Yes to God,* treats a modern and universal way of understanding and living God's will in today's society. The second, *The Word of Life,* speaks of the special attention given to putting the word of God into practice and singles out its many fruitful effects on both individual and group levels, while the third, *The Eucharist,* gives a profound explanation of this sacrament as the "bond of unity." Throughout these works, along with recounting her own experience, Chiara often quotes the saints, the popes, and the fathers of the Church.

The Editor

PART I
OUR YES TO GOD

HUMANITY'S "YES" TO GOD IN THE OLD AND NEW TESTAMENTS

The purpose of this book is to examine in depth one of the key points of the spirituality of the Focolare: God's will. We will look at what the Bible says about it; we will reflect on what we have understood about it through the life of the Focolare; and we will consult the statements and writings of some of the Church Fathers, a number of saints, the recent popes, and the Second Vatican Council. Let us begin by considering several fundamental passages in the Old and New Testament.

The essential relationship between God and each human being

In order to understand what the Scriptures reveal to us about God's will, we must first look at the type of relationship that existed between God and the human race in the Old Testament.

Since God created the human race, each person is a creature and, as such, is completely dependent upon God. This is the basic relationship, the first thing we should keep in mind. All that a human being is and does, he or she is and does as a creature.

In creating the human race, however, God made human beings different from other creatures; he made them, as we know, in his own "image and likeness" (Gn 1:26). But what does this really mean? It means that each human being is capable of a direct, personal relationship with God, a relationship of knowledge, love, friendship, and communion. It means that God created human beings as persons he can relate to, whom he can address as "you." As the theologian Westermann says, "Man's very essence is seen in his being 'face to face' with God. The relationship with God is not something added to human nature, rather man is created such that his human nature is understood within his relationship with God."[1]

This relationship with God is what makes us human. That is how we have been created.

An existential relationship with God

Since the essential characteristic of human nature lies in this relationship with God (inasmuch as being human consists in being God's image) then we must develop this relationship and live it out in our day-to-day lives if we wish to reach self-fulfillment. We have been created in this relationship with God; therefore, we can find fulfillment only within the context of this relationship.

The deeper our rapport with God becomes and the more it is lived and enriched, the more we ourselves are fulfilled and happy. By adhering to what God wants from us, to his plan for us, and by conforming our will to his, we reach our fulfillment as human beings.

God's "yes" to the human race

God's special concern for the human race did not end with its creation, but has continued down through the ages. We see this in the Old Testament where the question is posed: "What is man?" The psalmist asks God: "What is man that you care for him [literally: that you visit him]?" (Ps 8:5). Man can be properly understood, therefore, only as someone whom God is mindful of, whom God lovingly visits. Again the psalmist asks: "O Lord, what is man that you regard him [literally: that you know him], or the son of man that you think of him? Man is like a breath, his days are like a passing shadow" (Ps 144:3-5).

Even though we are mere transitory beings, God cares for us, knows us, listens to us. Although we are destined to die, we belong to God.

In the Bible, the human race as well as each individual person is always considered as belonging to God and dependent on him. There is no way for anyone to escape from the presence of God — from him each of us has come, and before him alone our ultimate destiny will be decided.

Some people seek the basis for human dignity in the spiritual side of human nature or in other human values. The Bible shows us, however, that human dignity is based on the fact that God cares for the human race and for each human being, and that in the course of human history he visits us, meets us, and redeems us. And it is precisely because of this encounter with God, that the human race has a future and can look forward to it with hope.

This, then, is God's side of the relationship, his "yes" to the human race. But what has been humanity's response?

Humanity's "no" to God

God's "yes" to the human race when he created it was a definitive "yes." Not even humanity's "no" could cause it to waver.

Genesis tells of God's love for the human race, of how he surrounds the first human beings with signs of his benevolence, and puts them in a delightful garden. Even the command not to eat "of the tree of the knowledge of good and evil," can be counted among these good gifts, for it is out of love that God warns them, "...in the day that you eat of it you shall die" (Gn 2:17).

But Adam and Eve violate God's command. Instead of complying with his will and accepting the fact that they are creatures, they try to assert themselves and become like God, not only ignoring him but turning against him. In them, all humanity attempts to overstep its limits, and to claim privileges that belong to God alone.

Created to be in relationship with God, called to respond with its "yes" to God's "yes," humanity answers instead, from the very beginning, with a refusal, with sin, with a "no."

God's judgment and God's mercy

Naturally, God's reaction to sin can be nothing other than a judgment condemning it, because sin is a serious matter. However, God does not abandon the human race. He punishes humanity, but he also saves it and sustains it. He expels Adam and Eve from the garden, but leaves them the gift of life; he drives Cain from the fertile land, but marks his forehead with a sign of protection. He sends the flood, but saves one family to be the ancestors of a new humanity, and promises them the stability of the natural order.

Thus the grace of God is greater than judgment.

Humanity's "yes" to God

Then God chooses Abraham, and in him the human race finally says its "yes" to God. "Now the Lord said to Abram, 'Go from your country and your kindred and your father's house to the land that I will show you. And I will make of

14

you a great nation, and I will bless you' " (Gn 12:1-2). And Abraham obeys: "So Abram went, as the Lord had told him" (Gn 12:4).

In choosing Abraham God is not choosing the Israelites alone, for in Abraham God sees all peoples: "In you all the families of the earth shall be blessed" (Gn 12:3).

God's plan for humanity

Humanity's acceptance of God's call ushers in a whole new era. Abraham is now guided by God. He no longer bases his life on his own ideas, but on God's will. And God's plan for him and for all humanity begins to unfold.

Abraham's acceptance means that he must follow God's commands. And God initiates him into an adventure that leaves him no respite and continually calls him to new and ever higher goals.

Genesis presents Abraham in all his greatness, but also in his weakness. Despite his limitations, however, his "yes" allows God to carry out his plans.

This experience makes it possible for Abraham — and therefore the whole human race — to begin an ascent to ever-more-noble religious, moral, spiritual, and social heights. In following God, Abraham will have a future he never dreamed of, because God has promised it to him and God is faithful to his word.

Thus God's entry into Abraham's life is like a new beginning for human history, and it directs all of history toward one end: the definitive coming of the kingdom of God through Jesus.

The God of Israel is first and foremost a personal God, as he reveals by his name, "I am who I am" (Ex 3:14), and by his desire for a covenant with the human race throughout the Old Testament. He addresses himself personally to the

15

Israelites and continues to address himself personally to every human being; and from all he demands an equally personal response.

On Mount Sinai God reveals his will to Moses in the Ten Commandments. God says that he himself took the initial step by rescuing the Hebrews from their slavery in Egypt; now he asks that they respond to his saving deed by observing his Law.

This revelation confirms Israel as God's chosen people and Israel celebrates it as a very great event.

In the first part of the Decalogue, we find the most important laws for the Israelite community—those concerning its relationship with God. In the second part, there is a summary of the fundamental human rights—the right of life, to a family, and so forth—and the duties that correspond to these rights.

Therefore, the existence of the people of Israel as the community of God's people requires two essential dimensions: one "vertical," their relationship with Yahweh, their God; and the other "horizontal," their relationship with one another and with all their fellow human beings. This horizontal relationship now takes on new importance because it is commanded by God as part of one's relationship with him. Thus, in a very basic way, the Ten Commandments safeguard the true concept of what it means to be human.

True "images of his Son"

Let us now move on to the New Testament. We have seen that God has created us in his image and likeness, and that therefore the way for us to become what we were meant to be, and to reach fulfillment as human beings, is to live according to his image and likeness.

In the New Testament, now that God has sent us his Son, Jesus—who is God, yes, but God made man—for us to be like

16

God, to conform ourselves to his image, means to conform ourselves to Jesus, or as Paul would say, "to be conformed to the image of his Son" (Rm 8:29). In the Son we reach our fulfillment as children of the Father, even to the point of perfect likeness with God in heaven.

Doing God's will brings us to fulfillment

From what has been said up to now, it is clear that carrying out God's will makes us free, makes us more and more our true selves. Obeying God and adhering to his will furthers our development as human beings, releases our creativity, and brings out our true personal identity.

Doing God's will, therefore, is not something unnecessary or artificial, or in conflict with being oneself. It is not a question of resigning ourselves to a more or less desirable fate. And it is still less a matter of forcing ourselves to undergo an unpleasant situation while thinking: "God has decreed it so. That is how it must be. It is inevitable."

Doing God's will is something altogether different: it is the best thing we could possibly desire for ourselves. It is what we have been created for.

By doing God's will we are helping ourselves and others to see his plan for each of us personally and to come to a fuller realization of his overall plan to bring all people to salvation and to the glory of heaven.

Jesus manifests God's will in its entirety

The Commandments of the Old Testament not only express God's will for us; they also express his love. He has given them to us for our good because he loves us. However, they do not express the whole of his will. His will is more complex, manifold — it goes far beyond the letter of the Law understood even

17

in its fullest sense.

In the fullness of time Jesus came to manifest God's will in its entirety. He did this in a total way, through his teaching and through his life.

His behavior—especially his giving of himself on the cross, which shows us the meaning of the love he taught—has become the norm for Christian behavior, a norm which cannot be completely codified because it is life and because it is love.

For a Christian, to do God's will means first of all to "live like Jesus," that is, to live in a loving filial relationship with the Father which is expressed by doing his will completely.

Jesus comes to complete the Law

Among the Jewish people, particularly after the exile, many felt that to be as close as possible to what God wanted them to be, they had to know and observe all the precepts and restrictions of the Law to the letter. But often this observance was so scrupulous that they lost sight of the foundation of the Law itself, that is, the relationship of love that each person must have with God.

Jesus, like the prophets, speaks out against this deformation of the Law.

Jesus has no intention of nullifying Scripture because for him, too, it is all God's Word. However, he says he has come to "fulfill" it (Mt 5:17).

Jesus tries to show through his actions how some precepts of the Law are to be interpreted. For example, he heals on the Sabbath—which appears to violate the Law—in order to explain that "the Sabbath was made for man, not man for the Sabbath" (Mk 2:27). He means by this that there is no need for people to become entangled in a thousand subtle distinctions regarding the Sabbath observance, because God has given the obligation of the Sabbath out of love for humankind. Thus he puts the Sabbath rest into its rightful perspective.

When questioned by some of the Pharisees and Scribes regarding "the tradition of the elders," and asked why his disciples do not observe this, Jesus reminds his questioners that they have subordinated God's will to their own tradition, and he reasserts the importance of God's commandment: "Honor your father and your mother" (Ex 20:12). For these Pharisees and Scribes asserted that those who offered God the money which would have been used to help their parents, were no longer obliged to assist them (cf. Mt 15:1-9).

In short, Jesus acts as one who has a direct and authentic knowledge of the will of God expressed in the Law. He thereby reveals that he is the true interpreter of the Law.

He interprets it most clearly in the Sermon on the Mount (Mt 5:21-48). There he refers to several commandments and customs, goes to their roots, and recasts them in that new form and with that fullness toward which the Law itself had been directed. It is not enough to refrain from killing; you must avoid anger toward your brother and sister. Besides not committing adultery, you must not even desire another woman. Not only must you not swear falsely, but you should not swear at all. Not "An eye for an eye and a tooth for a tooth," but "If anyone strikes you on the right cheek, turn to him the other also" (Mt 4:38,39). Not "You shall love your neighbor and hate your enemy," but "Love your enemies and pray for those who persecute you" (Mt 5:43,44).

Jesus wants to prevent the observance of God's commandments from being reduced to mere external acts; he wants our hearts to change. "There is nothing outside a man which by going into him can defile him; but the things which come out of a man are what defile him" (Mk 7:15). What is essential, therefore, is a personal relationship with God. And this is confirmed by what Jesus says with regard to charitable acts and acts of worship: they must be done not in order to "be praised by men," but as an expression of love for God (Mt 6:1-17).

God's will as presented by Jesus, therefore, does not abolish the Law, but reveals a deeper and fuller dimension of the Law.

Jesus takes the place of the Law

But in the fullness of time, the Law is no longer sufficient to express God's will in its entirety. What, then, is the will of God manifested by Jesus?

Announcing that the kingdom of God is near, Jesus warns us that we must convert in order to enter it. To convert means to leave everything, to sell everything in order to possess God, in order to enter his kingdom. We need only recall the parables of the hidden treasure and of the precious pearl, in which a man sells all he owns in order to buy them (Mt 13:44-46). The Christian must therefore love God more than father, mother, wife, husband, possessions — even more than life itself (Mt 19:29; Lk 14:26). Everything must be subordinated to God and be put aside for love of him — in a concrete way by some, in a spiritual way by all of us. Jesus invites each person to choose God in a total way.

He asks for more, therefore, than what the Law requires. Indeed, when he says, "Leave the dead to bury their own dead; but as for you, go and proclaim the kingdom of God" (Lk 9:60), he seems to be going against the Law which commands: "Honor your father and your mother."

Jesus takes the place of the Law.

For Christians, Jesus is the Law

For Christians, Jesus is the Ideal to follow. And to follow Jesus means to accomplish the Father's will perfectly, as he does. Jesus himself sums it up in the commandment: "Love one another as I have loved you. There is no greater love than

20

this: to lay down one's life for one's friends" (Jn 15:12-13*).

Jesus does not merely speak about this love which is God's will for the new era; he lives it to the utmost. He is the first to have this total love for God and neighbor which he requires of others. His way of living, his doing God's will in giving his life for others, is the new law which we must follow.

Toward our total fulfillment: our divinization

But Jesus does not simply ask us to imitate him in accomplishing the Father's will; he offers us something greater, much greater. Having infused love into our hearts through the Holy Spirit (cf. Rm 5:5), he can now make us sharers — as he says in his testament (cf. Jn 13-17) — in his own relationship with the Father, in the relationships that exist among the persons of the Trinity. And he wants this reality to spread into the relationships among people. In this lies the highest possible fulfillment — the "divinization" — of the individual human being and of humanity itself. As the Church Fathers say, God became a human being in order to make human beings God.

For the early Church Jesus was the Law

The meaning of Jesus' words was more deeply grasped by the early Church after his death and resurrection, because of the example of his life.

For the early Church, and for Paul in particular, the Christian's new life has Christ as its reference point: he is the incarnation of God's will for the Christian. Paul writes, "Welcome one another, therefore, *as Christ has welcomed you*" (Rm 15:7). "Walk in love, *as Christ loved us and gave himself up for us*" (Ep 5:2). "Your attitude must be *that of Christ*" (Ph

2:5*). Summing it up in a single phrase, he speaks of the "law of Christ" (Gal 6:2), that is, Christ as the law of a Christian.

God has placed his law in human hearts

In concentrating on the observance of the Law, there is a danger that one may come to regard the Commandments as external constraints, and consequently have a servile relationship with God and a legalistic approach to his word. On the other hand, there is also the risk of becoming too self-confident and proud of one's ability to observe the precepts of the Law.

In the new order, however, the words of Jesus, written in human hearts, cannot be considered as something imposed from without. They cannot give rise to a servile relationship with God, nor can they be an occasion for boasting about oneself. God himself, through the Spirit, has poured love into our hearts, and "love is the fulfillment of the law" (Rm 13:10). In this way, what God wants becomes what each person wants in the depth of his or her heart.

Seeking to know God's will

Whatever the situation, a Christian can always be sure that it is God's will to love. How to love in the particular circumstances of one's everyday life is something each person must discover. Each of us, therefore, must know how to seek out and discern God's will. Paul's advice in this regard is: "Do not conform yourselves to this age but be transformed... so that you may judge what is God's will" (Rm 12:2*).

His will can be discovered moment by moment, by listening to the voice of the Spirit within us and being docile to it. Paul writes to the Galatians, "Walk by the Spirit" (5:16), by which he means: be "led by the Spirit" (5:18).

So we must sharpen our supernatural sensitivity, the evangelical "instinct" that the Spirit has given us, which can be developed only by putting it to use.

Paul holds that two things are necessary in order to obtain this greater sensitivity to the voice of the Spirit. The first is to be part of a Christian community and to progress in living the life of mutual love within the community. "This is my prayer: that your love [that is, your Christian love lived in the community] may abound more and more in knowledge and depth of insight so that you may be able to discern what is best" (Ph 1:9-10*).

The second prerequisite is prayer, because the knowledge of God's will is also a gift. "We have not ceased to pray for you, asking that you may be filled with the knowledge of his will" (Col 1:9).

The Commandments and the will of God

Since each Christian has the law of the Spirit in his or her heart, we might wonder whether the Commandments are still useful as rules of conduct to help us carry out God's will.

They are useful, indeed, because the law of the Christian is love and love is difficult to codify. We know how easy it is to confuse our own opinions and desires with the voice of the Spirit within us, and how easy it is, as a consequence, to act in a purely subjective manner, following our own feelings and inclinations.

Given our human, earthly condition, love needs to be explained and guided by objective norms which make its practical application easier and serve as sure points of reference.

Seen in this light, the Commandments become an aid for loving God and neighbor. And we Christians, convinced of this, should seek to understand the purpose behind each norm, the reason for its existence, in order to conform ourselves to the loving intention of the One who formulated it. Thus the written Law becomes a precious means put at our disposal. It is not, however, the goal of our lives.

For God's will is not that we obey a code of ordinances, but that we love him and our fellow human beings; and in this lies the fulfillment of the Law.

GOD'S WILL IN THE SPIRITUALITY
OF THE FOCOLARE

We must be truly thankful to God for the many insights he has given us with regard to this very important aspect of Christian life, particularly at the beginning of the Focolare, when he made use of providential circumstances to enlighten us, and suggested simple and effective examples that helped us to understand and do his will.

So that this wealth of experience may become the heritage of each member of the Focolare, I think it is appropriate for us to look back at the early days, for I am reminded of the words of Scripture: "Recall the former days...after you were enlightened..." (Heb 10:32).

Not those who say, "Lord, Lord," but those who do the Father's will

We had chosen God, who had manifested himself for what he is: Love. And we asked ourselves, "How can we love God with all our heart, with all our strength?" Then we remembered the words of Scripture, "Not every one who says to Me, 'Lord, Lord,' shall enter the kingdom of heaven, but he who does the will of My Father" (Mt 7:21). So we understood that to *love God* with all our heart, all our soul, all our strength, we had to *do his will* with all our heart, all our soul, all our strength.

It was clear, therefore, that loving God was not a matter of experiencing some particular sentiment, but of doing his will.

25

To do his will became the practical way of showing our love for him.

We realized that we possessed a great gift—our free will—and that nothing could be more reasonable for us human beings, children of God, than to freely put our freedom at the service of the One who had given it to us. Thus from that moment on, we resolved to do not our own, but God's will.

We immediately sought to unite our will to his. Our only will now was to do his will. In this way we would be truly loving him.

The state of perfection vs. perfection

At about that same time—I do not remember whether before or after—an experience of mine helped us to understand something very important. In December of 1943, God had called me to consecrate myself to him with a vow of chastity. Then, during midnight Mass on Christmas of the same year, I felt in my heart that Jesus was asking me to give him *everything*. By "everything" I naturally understood what most people in my situation would have understood at that time: that in addition to the vow of chastity, I should give God my own will through the vow of obedience and all that could be considered mine through the vow of poverty, and that I should leave my family and the beautiful things of the world by entering a cloister—the strictest form of cloister. I said "yes" to God, although I wept and was in torment because of something rebelling within me.

The next day I went to my confessor, and since he knew of the life that was springing up around me—I had already been joined by my first companions—he said very decisively, "No. This is not God's will for you."

At that moment, two ideas which in my mind had previously coincided, became distinct: the so called *state* of perfection, and perfection. I understood then that although undoubtedly there were states of life that were more or less perfect, *perfection* could be attained only by doing God's will.

A way to holiness for everyone

I remember that until that moment I felt as if a high wall were blocking my way to holiness. And I had been trying to find a breach in that wall. I used to think: if it is a matter of doing penance, then we should wear hair shirts all day long and scourge ourselves till we bleed. Or if it is a matter of praying, we should pray all day long.... But the question still remained: "What must we do to become saints?" I simply did not know. It was principally through this experience I just mentioned, that God enlightened me, and I understood that to reach sanctity it is enough to do his will.

It was a wonderful discovery! And so practical too. Here was a way that was good for everyone: men and women, young and old, gifted and less gifted, intellectuals and laborers, mothers and those in religious life, lay people and clergy, government officials and ordinary citizens. Here was a way to sanctity wide-open to every human being. I felt I had in my hands the passport to perfection—not only for an elite group of persons called to the priesthood or religious life, but for the masses.

A divine adventure

I saw that two roads lie before us in life, and that my friends and I, like everyone else, would have to choose between them: we could spend this life either following our own will, or following God's will.

If we followed our own will, our destiny would be like that of almost everyone else in the world. Each day many people die, and the tears and flowers show that their death causes much suffering. But then, after another generation has passed, most of them have been forgotten.

If, instead, we walked the way of God's will, he would guide us moment by moment along paths conceived by his love, invented by his imagination, and suggested by his providence, which cares for each of us as individuals and for the community as a whole. He would lead us on a marvelous, divine adventure, as yet unknown to us. And our lives would not end in silence, but would remain to give light to many, like the lives of the saints.

We were so convinced that choosing God's will was the best, most worthwhile, beautiful, and beneficial thing to do, that we were struck by what we considered the strange way of reasoning of so many people who limit themselves to being resigned to God's will. We used to say: "What?... *Resign* ourselves to God's will? On the contrary! We should have to resign ourselves if we do our own dull will, so unprofitable and inconclusive!" We should *want* to do God's will because it is the greatest thing we could desire. And we should not say, "I *must* do God's will," but rather, "I *can* do God's will!"

Seen in this perspective, all our personal plans fell into insignificance and we abandoned ourselves completely to God.

We knew that God's will was a Father's will. We could place ourselves in his hands without fear. Certainly, anything that he willed would be for our good.

We believed in love.

This complete trust in God did not mean we became passive. Quite the contrary: once we had grasped God's will, we made it our own and carried it out with all our heart, with all our soul, with all our strength, endeavoring to be as faithful to it as possible even though it was constantly changing.

When we did not know what God wanted, we did what we thought best, asking God to put us back on the right track

28

if we had made the wrong choice.

Before long, we had acquired a considerable amount of the flexibility one must have in order to be able to understand his will.

We knew that by living this way we were putting into effect a divine plan, about which we knew nothing except that we were being guided by God, our Father, and that every circumstance was an expression of his love for us.

Jesus: our model in doing the Father's will

Living like this, we were struck by many passages of Scripture. Jesus had said, "My food is to do the will of him who sent me" (Jn 4:34), and we wanted to be able to say the same. He had also said, "I have come down from heaven, not to do my own will, but the will of him who sent me" (Jn 6:38). "Nevertheless not my will, but yours, be done" (Lk 22:42). "I always do what is pleasing to him" (Jn 8:29). "I have come to do your will, O God" (Heb 10:7).

Jesus was our example. We imitated him, not in an exterior way—as, for example, in his scourging or in going without a traveling bag—but in the fact that, like him, we wanted to do God's will. This is reflected in the following passage from a meditation I wrote in 1946.

> Each of us must aim at being another Jesus as soon as possbile; we must act as Jesus here on earth....
>
> We must put our human nature at God's disposal so that he can use it to make his beloved Son live again in us.
>
> In order to do this we should do only God's will, as Jesus did.
>
> May we always be able to have on our lips the words Jesus used in reference to himself....
>
> When we have succeded in being able to be like Christ in his determined, total obedience to the Father, then we will experience inner unity.

29

Imitating the Saints

We viewed the saints from the same perspective. We were not to imitate them by mindlessly copying their actions, but by striving to do God's will as they had done.

How different they all were from one another; yet they were identical in one thing: they all had done God's will.

At that time our whole purpose in life was summed up in doing God's will. For example, being consecrated to God with vows was something important, but God's will was more important.

I remember that I considered my sister who was called to married life to be just as fortunate as I. I felt we were truly equal. I said to her: "You are getting married, and you are doing God's will. I will live a life of virginity. But we are equal because what is important is God's will."

To do God's will was the norm that bound us together as one family with Jesus our brother and God our Father.

Understanding God's will: the "new commandment"

We found God's will expressed for us above all in the new spirituality that was coming to life. We had chosen to live for God alone, and had understood that in order to be faithful to this choice, we had to put into practice the commandment that Jesus calls his own: the "new commandment" (cf. Jn 13:34; 15:12).

This commandment influenced everything we did. To carry it out as well as possible, we made a pact. And we recognized that even our love for Jesus Forsaken—that is, for Jesus in the moment of his greatest suffering when he cried out, "My God, my God, why have you forsaken me?" (Mt 27:46)—was an integral part of being faithful to this commandment. Moreover, it was living this command that brought about the unity willed by Jesus and that enabled us to have him present in our midst. And the desire to live this command well gave us added incentive to live all the other words of the Gospel.

God had focused our attention on the new commandment, and now we realize more and more that in so doing he had revealed to us the very heart of Christianity.

God's will was also manifested to us by the Ten Commandments, as well as by the precepts of the Church, by our superiors, and by the duties of our state in life. Even civil laws were an expression of God's will for us, as were life's various circumstances, whether they were joyful, sorrowful, or indifferent.

Listen to "that voice"[1]

We had a kind of compass for determining God's will. It was the "voice" within us, the voice of the Holy Spirit. We used to urge one another to listen to "that voice." At that time, for us to speak of a "voice" meant to risk being taken for heretics. And it was equally difficult for us as lay people to speak about the Gospel or about love.

We got used to listening to "that voice" in order to know God's will. Later on, in the light of this experience, we understood that one of the reasons why God had created the Focolare was that the presence of Jesus in the midst in the Focolare was like a loud-speaker that amplified God's voice within each one of us, enabling us to hear it more clearly. We often say that in the Focolare we live between two "fires": God within us and God in our midst. Here in this divine "furnace" we are formed and trained to listen to Jesus and to follow him. We are encouraged by the fact that St. Paul himself is clearly of the opinion that in order to understand God's will, a person should be part of a Christian community where Christ is alive and present (cf. Ph 1:9-10).

31

The present moment

At the beginning of the Focolare we were in constant danger of losing our lives, because we were not adequately sheltered during the air raids. So when the question arose as to when we had to do God's will in order to love him, we immediately understood that the answer was: now — right now. For we did not know if we would still be alive later.

The only time in our possession was the present moment. The past was already gone, and we did not know if the future would ever come. We used to say: "The past no longer exists; let's entrust it to God's mercy. The future is not yet here. By living the present, we will also live the future well when it becomes present."

We realized how foolish it was to live in the past, which will never return, or in the future, which may never come and which, in any case, is unpredictable.

We took the example of riding on a train. Just as a traveler remains seated and would not think of walking up and down the aisle in order to get to the destination sooner, so we had to remain in the present. The train of time moves ahead on its own.

Living the present, one moment after another, we will one day reach that decisive moment upon which our eternity depends. Having loved God's will in the present with all our heart, all our soul, all our strength, we will have fulfilled, throughout our lives, the commandment to love God with all our heart, all our soul, all our strength.

The expressed and unforeseen aspects of God's will

Employing a distinction used at the time, we noted the difference between the divine will already "signified" for us and the divine will of God's "good pleasure" not yet manifested to us; in other words, between what we might call

32

God's "expressed" will and his "unforeseen" will. God's expressed will included all that we *knew* we had to abide by: the Commandments, the word of God, the precepts of the Church, the duties of our state in life, etc. God's "good pleasure," on the other hand, referred to the various unforeseen aspects of his will which are made manifest to us through events and circumstances, such as an unexpected encounter, a fortunate occurrence, a tragedy, a new situation, etc.

We tried to carry out the expressed will of God as perfectly as possible, while maintaining the flexibility necessary in order to be able to change our course of action as soon as circumstances revealed that God wanted something different from us.

Among the first members of the Focolare some were inclined to be more attentive to one or the other of these expressions of God's will. We noted the positive and negative aspects of both attitudes, and we concluded that perfection consisted in being able to grasp what God wanted in the present moment, and doing it.

Those who were more inclined to carry out the expressed will of God, and less concerned with the unforeseen aspects of his will, tended not to notice when circumstances indicated a new course of God's will, and consequently they tended to have a less intimate relationship with him, not giving themselves to him with all their heart. So although they believed they were devoted to their duties, they were, in fact, devoted to themselves!

On the other hand, those who were more inclined to do God's will as manifested by circumstances had a greater appreciation of the "poetry" of the Gospel, and found it easier to see the "golden thread" of God's providence running through everything that happened. At times, however, aided by their imagination, they thought they saw God everywhere; and they presented the life of the Gospel in a way which was too adventurous and romantic. By so doing, they deprived the Gospel life of its most beautiful characteristic: the *normality* of a life that is supernatural, but simple; neither artificial nor excessive, but pure and harmonious — as nature is, as Mary is.

Consequently, we made a determined effort to become more and more adept at perceiving God's plan for each one of us in every present moment, and to truly *be* what he wanted of us, in each moment.

The ray of God's will

To illustrate how we wanted to live, we used the image of the sun with its rays. The sun was God, the rays his will. Each one of us, in each present moment of our life, had a ray of the sun to walk in, that is, God's will for him or her. Each person's ray was distinct from the others; yet all were rays of the sun, all were God's will. Therefore, all of us were doing only one will — God's will — but it was different for each person. Because of this one will — which bound us to one another, to Jesus, and to the Father — each one of us felt that he or she was one with each of the others, with Jesus, and with the Father.

As the rays of the sun are *one* with the sun, similarly, God's will coincides with God. Thus, by loving his will, we were loving him.

We had to follow our ray: always walking in it, always being enlightened by it — remaining constantly in God's will. To do this successfully, we needed to use violence at times in order to silence our own will and to hold fast to his, which is, after all, the expression of his love for us.

When we succeeded in doing his divine will consistently in many successive present moments, we experienced that his yoke was light and easy (cf. Mt 11:29).

Everything in our lives changed. For example, our relationships with others: previously we used to associate with people we liked, and we loved those whom we found pleasant. But now we were happy to seek the company of whomever God

34

willed us to be with, and we would stay with them for as long as he willed it.

The fact that we were completely intent upon doing God's will in each present moment led to our being detached from everything else, and from ourselves as well. This detachment was not something deliberately sought after—we sought God alone. It simply came as a consequence, because two things could not occupy our attention at the same time. Where there was the divine will, there was no room for ours. In the present moment we could not do two things at once. So rather than labor to eradicate our own will, we worked to acquire the divine will.

Getting back in our ray

Whenever we realized that we had "gone out of our ray," as we used to say, into the darkness, and had spent a few moments doing our own will and letting our old self[2] live, we knew the only way to improve the situation was to start doing the divine will of that present moment. Since we had not loved God in those previous moments, we had to love him at least in that present moment.

We felt that with each passing moment of each new day, we were adding stitches to a magnificent embroidery. Those moments which we had not spent "in our ray" were entrusted to God's mercy. To us, looking from below—from the under-side of the embroidery, as it were—those moments seemed like so many knots in the threads. But we knew that this was simply our human way of looking at things. We were certain that God's love mends every tear and binds every broken thread. And so we knew that, seen right side up—from God's vantage point—the design would turn out perfectly. And from heaven our lives would be seen as the wonderful stories of true children of God.

We liked very much something St. Francis de Sales had said about the relationship between Christians and God's will. It could be paraphrased in this manner: "True Christians will carry this name engraved in their hearts: 'I am God's will for me.' "[3]

All that God wills or permits is for our good

Everything that God asked of us was love. In each moment he came to us in his will; and whether this appeared beautiful or sad to us, it was nonetheless he himself coming to us with his love.

But how were we to consider the things he merely allowed to happen? What about our mistakes, our weaknesses? From the very beginning, Catherine of Siena was an encouragement to us in this regard, with her statement, "All that God wills or permits is for our sanctification."[4]

So we knew we should never let anything stop us. If we made a mistake, we could not let it discourage us. Whatever happened, if entrusted to God's mercy, would not only cease to be useless or harmful, but would help us to acquire humility, which is the foundation for sanctity.

In fact, Scripture says, "God makes all things work together for the good of those who love him" (Rm 8:28). We had wanted to love God, and we discovered that, as a result, everything that happened in life would contribute to our personal spiritual growth.

As we strove to do God's will, the Holy Spirit soon taught us that it was good to do the good that God wanted, but it was bad to do the good that God did not want. This understanding made our new life even more dynamic.

Doing God's will with all our heart, with all our mind and with all our strength brought us great peace and joy — peace and joy that the world cannot give, but that only God can

36

bestow.

Outside of God's will we found no light, no love, no peace—only torment.

Thus we learned to distinguish between natural and supernatural life. Even before then we had possessed supernatural life and God's grace, but we had not done enough to make this divine life bear fruit. Even though we were baptized we practically lived like pagans, because our hearts and minds were attached to many things instead of to God alone.

A new understanding of Mary

In living according to God's will we also came to a deeper understanding of Mary. We admired her as the most perfect creature who had ever lived on this earth, because she had done only God's will.

Therefore, if doing God's will meant "to live as Jesus," it also meant "to live like Mary": this was the best way to show our devotion to her and to be her children. We took as our own her words, "I am the servant of the Lord. Let it be done to me as you say" (Lk 1:38*).

God's plan for us: a new movement in the Church

But this effort to do God's will always, moment by moment, brought about another effect in our lives. Since in doing his will we were loving him, and he manifests himself to those who love him (cf. Jn 14:21), he manifested himself to us.

From the very beginning, and continuing down through the years to the present, the Holy Spirit has been gradually revealing to us the splendid plan God had for each one of us and for our group.

This divine plan has brought a new movement to life in the Church: a movement beautiful beyond words; sacred, like all that is both human and divine; alive, like the Body of Christ, of which it is an expression; and rich—infinitely rich—because it was designed in heaven. And urged on by its divine architect, the movement is intent upon resolving—together with other Christian movements—the most significant problems facing humanity today.

The Church has studied the Focolare, has blessed it and approved it, and has confirmed its life as being God's will for all who belong to it and all whom God will call to be part of it in the future.

THE CHURCH'S "YES" TO GOD
(Part One)

Scripture makes it clear that we should do God's will. And the saints also exhort us to do so. For example, Maximilian Kolbe writes to his mother in these words:

> I will wish you, Mother, neither health nor prosperity. Why? Because I want to wish you better than that, something so good that God himself would not wish you better: that in all things, the will of this very good Father be accomplished in you, Mother, that you may know in all things how to fulfill the will of God! This is the very best I can wish for you. God himself could not wish better than that.[1]

Let us now compare our own experience, point by point, with what we find in the Church Fathers, the saints, the popes and the Second Vatican Council.

Our will must coincide with God's will

The Lord made us understand that our will must coincide with his.

Francis de Sales says, "The soul that loves God is so transformed into the divine will that it merits, rather, to be called God's will than to be called obedient and subject to his will."[2] And a "precious grace" received by Catherine of Siena "was the conformity of her will with, and, as it were, the absorption of her will into, the will of God."[3] This transformation of Catherine's will was so perfect that she did not hesitate to write, even to the popes, "Thus you will do God's will and mine."[4]

Sanctity and God's will

It was clear to us from the very beginning that by doing God's will we could reach sanctity. The saints, too, say that perfection lies precisely in this.

Catherine of Siena, for instance, is convinced that whoever takes this road will travel swiftly from one virtue to the next. And she writes:

> O tender, loving Jesus, may your will be accomplished in us always, as it is in heaven by your angels and saints.... Then the soul...will run like an unbridled horse, from grace to grace, at full speed, and from virtue to virtue. It will no longer have any restraints to hold it back from running because it will have cut away from its own will every disordinate appetite and desire, for these are reins and fetters that obstruct the race of spriritual persons.[5]

Teresa of Avila, whose way to reach God was prayer, is of the same opinion. She has no doubt that perfection lies in doing God's will, and that the more one does so, the more graces one receives.

> All that the beginner in prayer has to do — and you must not forget this, for it is very important — is to labor and be resolute...to bring his will into conformity with the will of God.... This comprises the very greatest perfection which can be attained. The more perfectly a person practices it, the more he will receive of the Lord and the greater the progress he will make on this road.[6]

This is how she corrects those who think that perfection is to be found in mystical phenomena:

It will become quite clear that the highest perfection consists
not in interior favors, or in great raptures, or in visions, or in
the spirit of prophecy, but in the bringing of our wills into
conformity with the will of God.[7]

And she gives a personal example:

While I was wondering if the people were right who disap-
proved of my going out [to found monasteries] and if I should
do better to occupy myself continually in prayer, I heard these
words: "For as long as life lasts there is no gain to be had in
striving to [enjoy Me more], but only in doing My will."[8]

For Paul of the Cross, "The highest perfection consists in
being perfectly united to the Most Holy Will of God."[9] And
Paul VI tells us what holiness is in these words:

This holiness to which we are called, is the result of two
component factors, the first of which...is the grace of the
Holy Spirit.... To be in the grace of God is everything for us.
Our perfection is the possession of divine charity. [But] is there
nothing else to be done? Yes, another factor is necessary... if
we do not wish to fall into quietism or moral indifference. It
is our "yes"; it is making ourselves available for the Spirit, and
accepting—even more, desiring—the will of God....[10]

John XXIII affirms that "real greatness lies in doing the
will of God, entirely and perfectly."[11]

God's divine plan for us

As for us, from the very beginning we have always believed
that if we do God's will and not our own, then our lives will
be following the pattern of his divine plan.

Paul VI recalls the example of St. Joseph, who had such an
extraordinary destiny because he was always faithful and

41

constant in listening to the Almighty, and he comments:

> The splendid plans of God, the provident enterprises that the Lord has in mind for human destinies, can co-exist with and rise above the most ordinary conditions of life....
>
> To conform our capricious, obstinate, often mistaken, sometimes even rebellious will to his; to make this small but sublime will coincide...with the will of God... *is the secret to living a great life.* It is to merge ourselves with the Lord's thoughts and to enter the plans of his omniscience and mercy as well as of his immense generosity.[12]

Resignation to God's will

We have already seen that in the early days of the Focolare, the words "God's will be done" were definitely not an expression of mere resignation for us. To do God's will was our greatest joy, our greatest glory!

In his book, *The Way,* Josemaría Escrivá de Balaguer, founder of Opus Dei writes: "Resignation?... Conformity? *Love* the Will of God!"[13] And he sees four steps in the development of a Christian's spiritual life, which are, appropriately, "to be resigned to the Will of God; to conform to the Will of God; to want the Will of God; to love the Will of God."[14]

Likewise, for Paul of the Cross:

> It is great perfection to resign oneself in all things to the divine will; it is greater perfection to live with great indifference, abandoned to God's good pleasure; the greatest, highest perfection is to nourish oneself, in a pure spirit of faith and love, on the divine will.[15]

How to know God's will

As I described in the previous chapter, we wanted to know God's will and, from the start, we did our best to discover it.

When we had doubts about what to do in the present moment, we would decide on a certain course of action, asking God at the same time to put us back on the right track if we had made the wrong choice.

John of the Cross has something beautiful to say in this regard. He suggests that spiritual persons can obtain light and guidance from two sources: "natural reason and the law and doctrine of the Gospel."[16]

Elizabeth of the Trinity reminds us that God's will is also contained in the Rule the Church has given us. "From the morning to night, the Rule is there to express God's will for us moment by moment. If you only knew how I love this Rule which is the form in which he wants me to reach sanctity."[17]

Jesus: our model in doing God's will

From the very first days of this new life, the Holy Spirit made us see clearly that Jesus was the one who had perfectly accomplished God's will.

This is confirmed by Paul VI:

> If the break in the life-giving relationship between God and mankind resulted from an act of rebellion on the part of man, eager for an independence that was to be fatal to him, with the cry: "I will not serve" (Jr 2:20), reparation could only come through a contrary attitude, the one assumed by Jesus, the Savior, to whom, in the Letter to the Hebrews (10:5-7), the following words are attributed: "Coming into the world he said: '...Lo, I have come to do your will, O God...'" (cf. Ps 40:7-9).[18]
>
> One cannot understand and reconstruct something of the figure of Christ without regarding the essential importance which fulfillment of the Father's will assumes in him....[19]

All that Jesus did was done in order to obey the Father; he is our model. Moreover, he acted in such a way that we can imitate his example. Augustine points this out:

> "Father," he said, "if it be possible, let this cup pass from me." This was the human will which wanted something of its own.... But...he added, "nevertheless, not as I will, Father, but as you will" (Mt 26:39).... Therefore, that you might want something different from what God wants is permitted because of human frailty...it would be most unusual if you did not want some particular thing. But immediately reflect on the One who is above you. He is above you, you are below him; he is the Creator, you are the creature; he is the Lord, you are the servant.... That is why he corrects you, why he causes you to submit to the Father's will, saying on your behalf: "Nevertheless, not as I will, Father, but as you will."[20]

John of the Cross reflects upon our desire to know God's will and then, "comparing the age of the written Law of the Old Testament with the age of the law of the Gospel and of grace, he warns us against desiring to be advised of God's will through extraordinary revelations and oracles accompanied by visions and voices. Even though such ways of knowing God's will were legitimate under the Old Covenant, they are no longer legitimate now."[21] The reason he gives for this conclusion is simply splendid!

> Now that the faith is established through Christ, and the Gospel law made manifest...there is no reason for inquiring of him in this way, or expecting him to answer as before. In giving us his Son...he spoke everything to us at once....[22]

Jesus, therefore, *is* the Father's entire message to us. In him, in his life, and in his teachings, we find what we must do. Writing in the third century, Cyprian put it this way:

> God's will is what Christ both did and taught: humility in behavior, firmness in faith, modesty in words, justice in deeds, mercy in works, uprightness in morals. It is to not even know what it means to do injury to another; it is to bear insults

patiently, to maintain peace with the brethren, to love God with all one's heart, to love him as Father and to fear him as God. It is to put aside everything for Christ because he put aside everything for us, to remain inseparably united to his love, to stay close to his cross...and, when the time comes to fight for his name...to be steadfast and open in giving witness to him, confident in the midst of torture, and patient in accepting the death for which we will receive the crown. This...is what it means to accomplish the Father's will.[23]

The saints — all different, yet alike in accomplishing God's will

We observed that the saints were so different from one another that each seemed a masterpiece, a unique creation of God's imagination. Yet they were all alike in that each had accomplished God's will. We have countless examples to choose from, but let us take Thérèse of Lisieux. Doing God's will was the dominant theme in her life:

> I desire only his will.[24]
>
> My God, "I choose all!" I don't want to be a saint by halves, I'm not afraid to suffer for you, I fear only one thing: to keep my own will; so take it, for "I choose all" that you will![italics added][25]

A few months before her death she declared:

> My heart is filled with God's will, and when someone pours something on it, this doesn't penetrate its interior; it's a nothing which glides off easily, just like oil which can't mix with water.[26]

One of those present during her last agony tells us that the prioress, Mother Marie de Gonzague, asked her: " 'And if it were God's will to leave you on the cross for a long time, would you accept it?' With extraordinary heroism she said: 'I would.' "[27]

45

Because she had lived this way, at the end of her life she was able to make the extraordinary statement: "In heaven the good God will do all I wish, because I have never done my own will upon earth."[28]

Where we find God's will expressed

Let us now consider where, and by whom, we find God's will expressed. We have repeatedly seen that, first of all, we find God's will in Jesus: he is *the* model of Christian behavior. Furthermore, he is also the revelation of God's will for every person on earth: he tells us what God wants from us as human beings.

The Second Vatican Council reminds us that " 'God our Savior... wishes [and, thus, Jesus wishes] all men to be saved and to come to the knowledge of the truth' (1 Tm 2:3-4)."[29]

The Council further declares that all human beings are called to be one people and that this likewise is God's will.

> All men are called to belong to the new People of God. Wherefore this People, while remaining one and unique, is to be spread throughout the whole world and must exist in all ages, so that the purpose of God's will may be fulfilled. In the beginning God made human nature one. After his children were scattered, he decreed that they should at length be unified again (cf. Jn 11:52).[30]

Another aspect of God's will expressed in the Gospel is that we should see and love Jesus in all persons. The Last Judgment will be based on this point. The Council clearly affirms: "The Father wills that in all persons we recognize Christ our brother and love him effectively in word and in deed."[31]

God also wants the unity of all Christians as brothers and sisters. In the words of John Paul II, "The will of Christ impels us to work earnestly and perseveringly for unity with all our Christian brethren...."[32]

We find God's will manifested in each day's events and situations, and in the responsibilities and circumstances of each of our lives. In this regard, the Council says:

> All of Christ's faithful, therefore, whatever be the conditions, duties, and circumstances of their lives, will grow in holiness day by day through these very situations, if they accept all of them with faith from the hand of their heavenly Father, and if they cooperate with the divine will.[33]

Christians must also read the will of God in the "signs of the times." This expression was frequently used by John XXIII and by the Council to indicate those events in which a Christian, enlightened by faith, can discern God's will in the course of history.

> The People of God believes that it is led by the Spirit of the Lord, who fills the earth. Motivated by this faith, it labors to decipher authentic signs of God's presence and purpose in the happenings, needs, and desires in which this People has a part along with other men of our age. For faith throws a new light on everything, [and] manifests God's design. . . .[34]

We also find God's will expressed in the commands which Jesus has given us.

And lastly, God's will is manifested to us by our superiors. Christians must look upon the words of the bishops as an expression of God's will because the bishops represent Christ. This is underscored by the Council:

> In the bishops. . .Our Lord Jesus Christ is present in the midst of those who believe. . . . Bishops in an eminent and visible way undertake Christ's own role as Teacher, Shepherd and High Priest. . . .[35]

Paul VI points out that authority in the Church is not self-constituted but was instituted by Christ who said, "Who hears

47

you hears me" (Lk 10:16).[36] And in its decree on the religious life, the Council says:

> Religious, therefore, should be humbly submissive to their superiors, in a spirit of faith and of love for God's will, and in accordance with their rules and constitutions. They should bring their powers of intellect and will and their gifts of nature and grace to bear on the execution of commands and on the fulfillment of the tasks laid upon them.... In this way, far from lowering the dignity of the human person, religious obedience leads it to maturity by extending the freedom of [the children of God].[37]

The saints regard the word of one's spiritual director or confessor as God's will. In the diary of Veronica Giuliani we read:

> Whenever I thought the Lord was commanding me to do something and was saying that this was what he wanted, and that on his behalf I should say this to the one who represented him, I would tell this to my confessors. But they almost always contradicted me.... Nevertheless, this gave me peace, for I felt that I could recognize God's will even more in what my confessor commanded than in what I had received in prayer.[38]

Listen to "that voice"

The compass that indicated God's will to us was "that voice," the voice within us, the voice of the Spirit. For with the coming of Jesus, God has written the law—which is his will—in our human hearts.

Paul exhorts us to "walk by the Spirit" (Gal 5:16), and he says that "all who are led by the Spirit of God" are children of God (Rm 8:14).

The Spirit is able to speak to us in a unique way; that special voice can be heard in our hearts.

48

At this point, however, we might wonder how non-Christians are able to discern God's will. In this regard, the Second Vatican Council states that, in addition to Divine Revelation, there is another privileged means for perceiving God's will which every person possesses: conscience.

> In the depths of his conscience, man detects a law which he does not impose upon himself, but which holds him to obedience. Always summoning him to love good and avoid evil, the voice of conscience can when necessary speak to his heart more specifically: do this, shun that. For man has in his heart a law written by God... (cf. Rm 2:14-16).[39]

Here is what Paul VI says about this voice:

> Is there a duty that exists independently of the obligations deriving from the laws of society? Yes, there is; and it springs from within us: it is the voice of conscience. We all hear it and it says to us: "You must!..." But this is not simply an innate impulse, a part of our psychological makeup: its source is a higher principle, a transcendent will, which re-echoes within us, interpreting and guiding our being in conformity with the divine mind. For God wants us to be as he conceived us to be, so that we may reach the fullness of our true nature, a nature that is free and progressing, designed to lead us to our fulfillment and to the merging of our lives with his wise and loving plan.[40]

The present moment

The Lord taught us to live the present moment in various ways. In the Gospels, for instance, it is evident that we should live the present moment. For we find there that we are to ask the Father for bread only for "this day" (Mt 6:11); we are told, "Today has troubles enough of its own" (Mt 6:34*); and we are warned: "No one who puts his hand to the plow and looks back is fit for the kingdom of God" (Lk 9:62).

The saints, too, encouraged everyone to live the present moment. Catherine of Siena used to say, "The fatigue of the past is no longer ours, because its time has gone; what is to come we do not possess, because we are not sure if its time will ever come."[41]

Another saint who stands out in this regard is the third century abbot, Anthony. One of the principal points in his teachings was: to begin anew "today," in purity of heart and obedience to God's will. This is brought out in his biography, written by Athanasius of Alexandria.

> He himself took no account of the time which had passed, but day by day, as if beginning his ascetical life anew, he made greater efforts to advance, constantly repeating to himself Saint Paul's saying, "I forget the past and I strain ahead for what is still to come" (Ph 3:13-14). He also recalled the words of the Prophet Elias who said, "As the Lord lives, whom I serve, I shall present myself before him today!" (1 K 18:15).[42]

Thérèse of Lisieux is an expert on how to live the present moment.

> Let us turn our single moment of suffering to profit, let us see each instant as if there were no other. An instant is a treasure....[43]
>
> My life is a flash of lightning, an hour that passes, a moment that fast escapes me and is gone. *My God, you know that to love you on earth I have nothing but today!*[44]
>
> A moment at a time, you can endure quite a lot.[45]
>
> I'm suffering only for an instant. It's because we think of the past and the future that we become discouraged and fall into despair.[46]
>
> This isn't like persons who suffer from the past or the future; I myself suffer only at each present moment. So it's not any great thing.[47]

Frances Xavier Cabrini wrote this beautiful piece of advice in one of her letters:

> Now what is done is done. Do not live in the past but in the present, and always look ahead to see what virtues you should practice in order to become a saint, a great saint, and soon too.[48]

And the popes are of one mind with the saints. John XXIII lived by the following norm:

> I must do everything, say every prayer, obey the Rule, as if I had nothing else to do, as if the Lord had put me in this world for the sole purpose of doing that thing well, as if my sanctification depended on that alone, without thinking of anything else.[49]

THE CHURCH'S "YES" TO GOD
(Part Two)

The expressed and unforeseen aspects of God's will

At the beginning of the Focolare, as I have mentioned, we saw that some aspects of God's will are clearly expressed, among other ways, in the Commandments, the words of Jesus, the duties of our state in life, and that other aspects of his will are unforeseen and are made known to us through circumstances.

Francis de Sales, a great saint and doctor of the Church, describes these two aspects of God's will in his *Treatise on the Love of God*. In book eight of the *Treatise* he explains that we show our adherence to the expressed will of God by being faithful to the Commandments, docile to the evangelical councils and to inspirations, and obedient to the Church and to our superiors.

In book nine he speaks of God's will as it is manifested to us by circumstances, and he says that our conformity to God's will in these instances is shown by our accepting the tribulations that God permits, but even more so by our practice of "holy indifference,"[1] that is, by our being totally available for whatever God may want.

Teresa of Avila manifests this "indifference," or better still, this complete abandonment to God's will, in a poem she wrote, whose refrain is: "What do you wish to do with me?" Here are a few verses:

I am yours, I was born for you—
What do you wish to do with me?

Give me life or give me death,
Give me sickness, give me health,
Give me strength or make me weak;
Give me war or perfect peace,
Revered by all or in disgrace,
I say my "yes" to all you choose.
What do you wish to do with me?

Give me wealth or make me poor,
Give me comfort, leave me sad,
Give me sorrow, give me joy;
Give me hell or grant me heaven,
A sweet life in the sun's pure light—
For I surrender all to you.
What do you wish to do with me?

If you wish, permit me to pray,
If you do not, let me be dry;
Make me fruitful and devout,
Or, if you wish, a barren land.
Sovereign Lord, in your will alone
Can I possess true peace.
What do you wish to do with me?

* * * * *

I am yours, I was born for you—
What do you wish to do with me?[2]

When Augustine speaks of God's will as manifested to us
by circumstances God permits, he acknowledges that we must
do our best to lessen the annoyance and discomfort which
accompany illness and misfortune, and that we may also seek
a way out of such situations. But he reiterates that whatever
the divine will disposes represents our true good.

Hence, if anything befalls us contrary to what we pray for, by bearing it patiently, and giving thanks in all things, we should never doubt that we ought to ask what the will of God intends and not what we will ourselves. For our Mediator gave us an example of this when he said, "Father, if it be possible, let this chalice pass from me," then, transforming the human will... he added immediately, "Nevertheless, not as I will but as you will, Father" (Mt 26:39).[3]

By putting the divine will before his human will, man rises from the human to the divine.[4]

Of course, all of us constantly aspire to enjoy peace and health and to be able to work. But what truly counts is God's will. And it is above all by doing the divine will that we contribute to the progress of the Church.

In every age and in many ways the saints have made clear that, no matter what, God's will is always our greatest good, even if it is painful. Augustine asks, "What does God want from you, or what does he demand of you, if not what is for your good?"[5] And elsewhere he adds:

The upright of heart are those who in this life follow God's will. The divine will is that at times you should be healthy, at times ill. If, when you are healthy, God's will is pleasant for you, and it is bitter, instead, when you are ill, you are not upright of heart. Why? Because you refuse to conform your will to God's will, but rather you want to bend God's will to fit your own.[6]

God's will and suffering

The saints are so conscious of the value of suffering in this life and they have so often experienced that God "disciplines" and "chastises" those he loves (Heb 12:6),[7] that in suffering they see nothing but God's will. Teresa of Avila explains it in this way:

So I want you to realize...what you are giving him when you pray that his will may be done in you. Do not fear that he will give you riches or pleasure or great honors or any such earthly things; his love for you is not so poor as that!... Would you like to see how he treats those who make this prayer from their hearts? Ask his glorious Son, who made it thus in the Garden. Think with what resolution and fullness of desire he prayed; and consider the manner in which he was answered.

And she then goes on to speak of Jesus' death on the cross and concludes:

So this is what God gave to [the One he loved most], and from that you can understand what his will is.

These, then, are his gifts in this world. He gives them in proportion to the love which he bears us. He gives more to those whom he loves most, and less to those he loves least.[8]

For Paul of the Cross:

Whoever wants to be holy longs to follow in the footsteps of Jesus.... His food is to do in all things the most holy will of God. And since this is done more in suffering than in pleasure, because in pleasure one always becomes attached to one's own will, the true servant of God loves the bare cross, receiving it directly from the most pure will of the Lord.[9]

John Bosco considers obedience and putting up with cold, heat, wind, and all our everyday sufferings as the penance that God offers us to enable us to attain heaven. He tells us of this conversation he had with Dominic Savio:

Once I found him quite downcast, exclaiming, "Poor me!... The Savior says that if I don't do penance, I won't go to heaven; and I have been forbidden to do penance: so what heaven shall I have?"

"The penance that the Lord wants from you," I told him, "is

obedience. Obey and that is enough for you."

"Couldn't you allow me some other penance?"

"Yes, you are allowed the penances of bearing patiently whatever wrongs may be done to you, and of tolerating with resignation the heat, cold, wind, rain, fatigue, and all the discomforts and ailments God may be pleased to send your way."

"But we have no choice but to suffer these things."

"By offering to God what you must necessarily suffer, it becomes virtue and gains merit for your soul."[10]

Some further insights into how we ought to act in the midst of suffering are contained in the words of Elizabeth of the Trinity:

> ...everyone who desires to live in communion with him must imitate his example.... We must allow ourselves to be immolated by all that the Father wills, after the example of Christ whom we adore.[11]
>
> May his holy will be the sword which immolates you at every moment.[12]

And Josemaría Escrivá de Balaguer writes:

> You suffer and you want to bear it in silence. It doesn't matter if you complain—it's the natural reaction of our poor flesh—as long as your will wants, now and always, only what God wants.[13]

All that God wills or permits

The idea that everything that happens is for the best, has been of fundamental importance in the task that God has entrusted to us, to build up the Focolare. We understood that everything that happened—not only what God willed, but also whatever he permitted—was directed toward our sanc-

57

tification. Knowing this, we were able to exploit even our mistakes for the kingdom of God.

Once again we were enlightened by the words of Catherine of Siena: "The one who loves perfectly serves faithfully with a living faith, and truly believes that whatever God gives or permits is given only to sanctify us...."[14]

The fruits of doing God's will

Let us now consider what the saints say we will experience if we do God's will. Catherine of Siena writes that doing God's will brings peace and tranquility: "Do you want to have peace and tranquility? Then get rid of your will, because every suffering has at its root your own will."[15]

For Josemaría Escrivá de Balaguer, the result of doing God's will is happiness:

> The wholehearted acceptance of the Will of God is the sure way of finding joy and peace: happiness in the Cross. It's then we realize that Christ's yoke is sweet and that his burden is not heavy.[16]
>
> *So much do I love your Will, my God, that I wouldn't accept heaven itself against your Will—if such an absurdity could be.*[italics added][17]

In her book *The Foundations,* Teresa of Avila narrates an episode from which we can see that persons who do God's will make great spiritual progress.

> Only a few days ago I was speaking with someone who...for almost fifteen years had been kept so busy by obedience [and, therefore, by God's will]...that he could not remember in all that time having had a day to himself.... The Lord rewarded him...because, without realizing [how], he found himself in possession of that precious and very dear freedom of spirit found in [those who are] perfect and in

58

which, truly, one enjoys all the happiness that can be desired in this life. One so favored desires nothing and possesses everything, fears nothing and desires nothing: is not upset by trials, nor exalted by consolations....

The same thing happened...to a number of other persons I know. Some of them I had not seen for years—even for a great many years—and when I asked them what they had been doing, they would say they had spent all their time in occupations imposed upon them by obedience and charity. And yet I found them so far advanced in spiritual matters that I was astounded.[18]

For Vincent de Paul, the result of doing God's will is a continual celebration: "What greater consolation could there be than to do God's will? You who are in the habit of doing it know that it is a continual banquet."[19] He, too, notices considerable spiritual progress in those who persevere in doing God's will.

Observe...the Christian who has submitted to the Will of God...he can say with the prophet: "You have held me by my right hand; and by your will you have conducted me..." (Ps 73:23-24). God holds him, as it were, by the right hand...so that you will see him today, tomorrow, the day after, for a whole week, a whole year and, indeed, during his whole life, living in a state of peace and tranquility.... If you compare him with those who follow their own inclinations you will see all his actions resplendent with light and ever fruitful in results. A noteworthy progress may be observed in his person, a unique force and energy in his works. God gives a special blessing to all he undertakes....[20]

It is striking to see how much this saint insists that union with and abandonment to God's will is the best way, *the* way to holiness.

Very often we are not sure what it means to give glory to God and, consequently, we do not know how to go about it. Listen to what Vincent de Paul has to say:

God is more glorified by the practice of union with his will
than by all the other [practices]....[21]

[Doing God's will] gives glory to God by rendering him that
submission which the creature owes its Creator and, in addition, it gives him joy and pleasure; yes...it gives joy to God
and in it he takes delight.... [By doing God's will] you will
give joy to God...you will give joy to the angels who rejoice
at the glory which God derives from the obedience rendered
to his holy Will by a poor creature, and you will give joy to
the Saints, who participate in the joy of God.[22]

Paul of the Cross writes:

With regard to any kind of suffering due to aridity, desolation, abandonment, temptations or anything else, the short cut
to recovery is true and peaceful resignation to the divine will.[23]

So for medication I will give you the cure-all, which is total
submission to God's holy will, accepting everything as coming
directly from his loving hand.[24]

And Frances Xavier Cabrini offers this advice:

Begin today to conform yourselves to God's holy will....
Then you will begin to enjoy—even here on this miserable
earth—the indescribable happiness the saints possess in
heaven. And you will experience a peace, tranquility, and joy
that are truly heavenly.[25]

Louise de Marillac finds that even our physical health
benefits when we do God's will.

Your health will benefit much from peace and tranquility of
spirit, as well as from your completely abandoning all things
to divine providence and allowing yourself to be led by love for
God's holy will, which is one of the most necessary practices
I know of in order to reach perfection.[26]

Teresa of Avila says that if we do God's will we will receive great divine favors that will lead us forward in the mystical life.

> The more resolute we are in soul and the more we show him by our actions that the words we use with him are not words of mere politeness, the more and more does our Lord draw us to himself...and raise us above all petty earthly things, and above all ourselves, in order to prepare us to receive great favors from him, for his rewards for our service will not end with this life. So much does he value this service of ours that we do not know for what more we can ask, while his Majesty never wearies of giving. Not content with having made this soul one with himself... he begins to cherish it, to reveal secrets to it, to rejoice in its understanding of what it has gained and in the knowledge which it has of all he has yet to give it. He causes it gradually to lose its exterior senses so that nothing may occupy it. This we call rapture. He begins to make such a friend of the soul that not only does he restore its will to it but he gives it his own also. And these two wills will be very compatible, because, seeing that the soul does what he wants, he is glad to allow it to rule with him. He does what the soul asks of him.... As we say, the soul will command and he will obey....[27]

Mary and God's will

From the beginning of the Focolare, we regarded Mary as an outstanding example of what it means to do God's will.

Here is how Augustine explains Mary's true greatness and her true kinship with Jesus:

> When...they told Jesus, who was speaking with his disciples, that his mother and brothers were outside waiting, he replied: "Who is my mother, and who are my brothers?" And stretching out his hand toward his disciples he said, "Here are my mother and my brothers! For whoever does the will of my Father in heaven is my brother, and sister, and mother" (Mt

12:48-50). Therefore, Mary too was his mother, inasmuch as she did the will of the Father. It is this that the Lord wants to exalt in her: that she has done the Father's will; not that she has generated the flesh of the Word from her flesh....[28]

One person who really loves Mary is Maximilian Kolbe. In one of his letters he writes:

> With no qualms at all you may use the expressions: "I want to carry out the will of Mary Immaculate"; "May the will of Mary Immaculate be done"...because she wants what Jesus wants, and he wants what the Father wants.
>
> Certainly, by referring so unreservedly to her will, you are, by that very fact, declaring that you love God's will; and, at the same time, you are witnessing to the truth that her will is so perfect that it does not differ in any way from God's will. And you are glorifying God, Father and Son, for having created such a perfect human being, and for having made her his Mother.[29]

How to do God's will

When it comes to the question of how to go about doing God's will, Catherine of Siena says that "we must kill our own will—and not halfway, but completely."[30] Paul of the Cross declares: "Whenever we feel some desire arise...to do what, for the moment, is not within our power, we must immediately silence this desire in God's holy will."[31] And he writes the following to a married friend:

> You can best foster your desires to do good by reducing them to one alone, namely, to do in everything the most holy will of God...without neglecting in the slightest way, the obligations of your married state, since this is God's will: that you be perfect in the state of holy matrimony.[32]

62

John Paul II, speaking to the priests of the United States during his visit in 1979, explained that we must surrender ourselves to God's will:

> ...the surrender to God's call can be made with utmost confidence and without reservation. Our surrender to God's will must be total—the "yes" given once for all which has as its pattern the "yes" spoken by Jesus himself. As St. Paul tells us, "...I declare that my word to you is not 'yes' one minute and 'no' the next. Jesus Christ...was not alternatively 'yes' and 'no'; he was never anything but 'yes' " (2 Cor 1:18-19).[33]

Many of the saints also say that we must abandon ourselves to God's will. Elizabeth of the Trinity, for example, writes: "Yes...let us live for love, always surrendered, immolating ourselves at every moment, by doing God's will without searching for extraordinary things...."[34]

For years now, we have seen how helpful it is—as a way of doing the will of God well—to offer him, one by one, each action of the day, saying: "This is for you." It seemed evident to us that the inspiration to do so had come from the Holy Spirit, particularly in light of the way this practice was enthusiastically received by all the members of the Focolare. And now we find this confirmed by one of the saints—Vincent de Paul:

> ...I wish, however, that we accustom ourselves to the practice of offering to God all that we do and suffer, and say to him: "...I wish it, Lord...."
> ...How important it is...to accustom oneself to the frequent renewal of this special intention [by saying, "This is for you"], especially in the morning on rising.... Finally, we should aim at raising our hearts to him in our principal actions, that we may consecrate them to him entirely and do them in conformity with his Will.
> ...We shall by this means acquire new titles to love. And

love will make us persevere and advance in this holy practice. Practice. . . is necessary. You must put into practice what I have just told you, if you are to practice the Will of God properly.[35]

The importance of doing God's will

Since the saints realized the importance of doing God's will, they were quick to take advantage of any means that might help them to do so. Louise de Marillac, who founded the Sisters of Charity together with Vincent de Paul, is an example.

> On the feast of St. Sebastian, I felt prompted to give myself to God so that I might do his holy will all my life. And I offered him the inspiration he had given me: that is, to take a vow in this regard, as soon as I received permission.[36]
> *Holy will of my God, how reasonable it is that you should be perfectly accomplished! You are the food of the Son of God on earth and therefore you are also what sustains my soul which has received its being from God.*[37]

This saint, whose life was an outstanding example of Christian charity, made a pact with those who had chosen to live this life with her, that they would always do God's will.

> So that you may conform yourselves to God's holy will in everything, I remind you of the pact we made all together: to never find fault with the conduct of Divine Providence.[38]

Maximilian Kolbe states emphatically that whoever is convinced of the importance of God's will "does not become attached to his work, or to the place where he is, or even to his prayer life, but solely and exclusively to the will of God, to God through Mary Immaculate."[39]

Veronica Giuliani tells how important doing God's will was

for her, even in her mystical experiences:

> The Lord showed me two crowns, one of thorns and the other of jewels. It seemed to me that he was inviting me to tell him which of the two I wanted. I longed for the one of thorns; however, I left it up to his holy will. The Lord granted my desire and placed the crown of thorns on my head; and he offered the crown of jewels to the Blessed Virgin who was also present.
>
> Jesus was standing there holding a lily and a palm branch, and he told me to take one of them. On the lily was written, "Joys and consolations"; on the palm were written these very words, "Victories and battles." ...I desired the palm but I did not have the boldness to ask for it. All I did was to entrust myself to his divine will. He held out the palm to me, but when it was in my hands, it was no longer a palm, but became the cross.[40]

Veronica was a member of the Poor Clares, a cloistered Franciscan order. In the 22,000 pages that she wrote out of obedience, over a span of thirty-four years, the declaration of wanting to do God's will comes up hundreds and hundreds of times, not only during the most elevated mystical experiences but also as a fruit of these moments.

Francis de Sales advises us not to pay attention to things and events in themselves, but to the fact that they are God's will.

> Do not attach importance to the things you do in themselves, but think only of the honor that is theirs — no matter how insignificant they may be — because they are willed by God....
>
> Seek each day to make yourself more pure of heart. But to possess this purity, you must appraise and weigh all things on the scale of the sanctuary, which is nothing other than the will of God.[41]
>
> Lower yourself willingly to do those actions which, externally, are less important, when you know that God wants you

to, because it doesn't matter whether the actions we perform are great or small, as long as we carry out God's will. Aspire often to the union of your will with that of our Lord.[42]

And John Bosco adds: "Whoever does God's will in small things, is doing something great in God's eyes."[43]

The Curé of Ars has these encouraging words to say, echoing what we have already heard from Teresa of Avila: "Jesus Christ shows he is ready to do our will if we begin to do his."[44] And if anyone says that doing God's will is difficult, Thérèse of Lisieux responds that God gives us the grace we need to do his will:

> Fortunately I didn't ask for suffering. If I had asked for it, I fear I wouldn't have the patience to bear it. Whereas if it is coming directly from God's will, he cannot refuse to give me the patience and the grace necessary to bear it.[45]

Pope John describes his own attitude toward God's will in vivid and effective terms:

> I live only to obey God's slightest commands. I cannot move a hand, a finger or an eye, I cannot look before me or behind, unless God wills it. In his presence I stand upright and motionless, like the lowliest soldier standing to attention before his officer, ready for [anything], even to cast myself into the flames.[46]

In speaking of priestly life, the Council makes a point which is valid for all of us: when we are faced with many things to do, what we must seek to do first is God's will.

> In today's world men have so many obligations to fulfill....As a result they are sometimes in danger of scattering their energies in many directions.
> For their part, priests [anxiously] seek for a way which will enable them to unify their interior lives with their program of

external activities.... [They] can truly build up this unity of life by imitating Christ the Lord.... His food was to do the will of him who sent him to accomplish his work (cf. Jn 4:34).[47]

Paul VI clarifies another aspect of God's will for us:

Everything in us that is necessary, compulsory and unchangeable leads us to realize and affirm that this is God's will. One person may be ill, another poor, still others may find themselves in tribulation and difficult situations. Then we bow our heads and exclaim with conviction: "Everything is disposed by the Lord!" And here a true dialogue with him can begin.[48]

The following splendid passage is also from Pope Paul. It is contained in his "Thoughts on Death."

And then—finally—an act of good will: which means not looking back anymore, but doing willingly, simply, humbly, and resolutely the duty resulting from the circumstances in which I now find myself because of your will.

I want to do quickly, perfectly, gladly, all you ask of me now, even if it far surpasses my strength and demands my life—finally, in this last hour.[49]

In a letter of Elizabeth of the Trinity we read:

...Our Lord...told us: "My food is to do the will of him who sent me" (Jn 4:34).

Hold fast therefore to the will of this adorable Master, look on every suffering as well as every joy, as coming directly from him, and then your life will be like a continual communion, for everything will be, as it were, a sacrament which gives you God himself. And that is perfectly true, for God cannot be divided; his will is his entire being.[50]

Yes, we must do God's will, and do it well, for all creation does so. Pope Clement of Rome wrote the following in a letter to his fellow Christians at the end of the first century:

> The heavens move at his direction and peacefully obey him. Day and night observe the course he has appointed them without getting in each other's way. The sun and the moon and the choirs of stars roll on harmoniously in their appointed courses at his command, and with never a deviation. By his will and without dissension or altering anything he has decreed the earth becomes fruitful at the proper seasons and brings forth abundant food for men and beasts and every living thing upon it. The unsearchable, abyssal depths and the indescribable regions of the underworld are subject to the same decrees. The basin of the boundless sea is by his arrangement constructed to hold the heaped up waters, so that the sea does not flow beyond the barriers surrounding it, but does just as he bids it.[51]

Therefore, if everything around us does God's will, so too must we. Peter Chrysologus is another who encourages us to do so:

> "His will be done on earth as it is in heaven" (cf. Mt 6:10). *On earth as it is in heaven:* when everyone will savor and carry out the will of God alone, then everything will be heaven...then all will be in Christ and Christ will be in all. Then all will be one—indeed, one single [Christ]—when the one Spirit of God lives in all.[52]

Doing God's will makes us one with him and one another

To conclude, I think it would be useful to read a letter that dates back to the beginning of the Focolare, to Christmas of 1946: it is our small echo to humanity's "yes" to God.

> Yes! Yes! Yes! A vigorous, total, determined, creative "yes" to God's will! We want to arrive at the Christmas crib loaded with gifts.

With all the ardor our hearts possess, let us say "Yes!" to God's will—always.

Why are we still so imperfect? Why still so many sins? Why aren't we all fused together in a single unity, whose splendid flower would be the fullness of joy and whose fruits would be...works for heaven?

Because we are still doing our own will!

If we all do the will of God, we will very soon be that perfect unity that Jesus wants on earth as in heaven!

Little sisters, far and near—all of you urged on by the same splendid idea—let's all gather at midnight Christmas eve, before the Christ Child, and then, recollected in profound prayer, let our hearts cry out "YES!"

I assure you that if we say it with all our heart, with all our mind, with all our strength, *Jesus will live again in us* and we will all be Jesus—Jesus who walks the earth again, doing good.

And isn't this our dream?

If, then, throughout our life, in each present moment, this "yes" is repeated with equal intensity, we will see that what we have so often asked for and so deeply desired as a Christmas gift—*to be Jesus*—will have come true!

I invite you all to do this, because over each one of us, God has placed a magnificent star—his particular will for each of us—and by following it, we will all arrive in heaven united, and we will see following in the wake of our own light, an array of other stars!

All that remains now is for each of us to heed this invitation and to say or renew our "yes" to God. May his will take root in each of our hearts and remain there always.

GOD'S WILL IN ALPHONSUS LIGUORI, DOCTOR OF THE CHURCH

In the course of this book I have not yet mentioned the teaching of Alphonsus Liguori regarding God's will, so that I might devote this chapter to his writings on the subject. I will be citing numerous passages from one of his works entitled, quite appropriately, *Uniformity with God's Will.*[1]

The spirituality of Alphonsus is centered on love for God, expressed in concrete terms as the uniting of our will to God's will. Thus, for Alphonsus, as for us, to love God means to do his will and, consequently, perfection lies entirely in doing God's will.

> Perfection is founded entirely on the love of God: *"Charity is the bond of perfection"* (Col 3:14), and perfect love of God means the complete union of our will with God's.... Mortification, meditation, receiving Holy Communion, acts of fraternal charity are all certainly pleasing to God—but only when they are in accordance with his will. When they do not accord with God's will, he not only finds no pleasure in them, but he even rejects them utterly and punishes them.[2]

We too have learned that we should do the good that God wants, and that to do the good that God does not want is bad. As Vincent de Paul says, "Good is bad when it is done where God does not want it."[3]

Alphonsus is impressed by how the saints have always done God's will:

71

To do God's will—this was the goal upon which the saints constantly fixed their gaze. They were fully persuaded that in this consists the entire perfection of the soul. Blessed Henry Suso used to say: "It is not God's will that we should abound in spiritual delights, but that in all things we should submit to his holy will." ...A certain Dominican nun was granted a vision of heaven one day. She recognized there some persons she had known during their mortal life on earth. It was told to her that these souls were raised to the sublime heights of the seraphim on account of the uniformity of their wills with that of God's during their lifetime here on earth.[4]

St. Vincent de Paul said, "Conformity with the will of God is the treasure of a Christian and the remedy for all evils, since it comprises self-denial, union with God, and all virtues."...

Some souls given to prayer, upon reading of the ecstasies and raptures of St. Teresa, St. Philip Neri, and other saints, wish that they also might come to enjoy these supernatural unions. Such wishes must be banished....If we really desire to be saints, we must aspire after true union with God which is to unite our will entirely to the will of God.[5]

According to Alphonsus, life *as it is in heaven* is the norm for our life on this earth:

During our sojourn in this world, we should learn from the saints now in heaven, how to love God. The pure and perfect love of God they enjoy there, consists in uniting themselves perfectly to his will. It would be the greatest delight of the seraphim to pile up sand on the seashore or to pull weeds in a garden for all eternity, if they found out such was God's will. Our Lord himself teaches us to ask to do the will of God on earth as the saints do it in heaven: *"Thy will be done on earth as it is in heaven"* (Mt 6:10).[6]

Alphonsus further states that "a single act of perfect uniformity with the divine will suffices to make a saint."[7] And he has consoling words for those who think they have little to give to God, little strength to love him because they are sick, and little to give to the poor, and are, therefore, tempted to envy those who are martyrs, missionaries, or heroes:

> He who gives his goods in alms, his blood in scourgings, his food in fasting, gives God what he *has*. But he who gives God his will, gives himself, gives everything he *is*. Such a one can say: "Though I am poor, Lord, I give you all I possess...."[8]

Alphonsus makes a distinction between *conformity* with the divine will and *uniformity* with the divine will.

> If we want to be completely pleasing to the heart of God, let us strive in all things to conform ourselves to his divine will. Let us not only strive to conform ourselves, but also to unite ourselves to whatever dispositions God makes of us. *Conformity* signifies that we join our wills to the will of God. *Uniformity* means more—it means that we make one will of God's will and ours, so that we will only what God wills; that God's will alone, is our will.[9]

Sometimes we are troubled by the things that happen to us or around us, because we do not know whether what is happening is God's will. But listen to what Alphonsus says:

> ...It is certain and of faith, that whatever happens, happens by the will of God.... And our Lord himself told St. Peter that his sacred passion came not so much from man as from his Father: *"Shall I not drink the cup which the Father has given me?"* (Jn 18:11).
>
> When the messenger came to announce to Job that the Sabeans had plundered his goods and slain his children, he said: *"The Lord gave and the Lord has taken away"* (Jb 1:21). He did not say "The Lord has given me my children and my possessions, and the Sabeans have taken them away."[10]

And those who live according to this conviction are greatly blessed by God:

Cesarius points up what we have been saying by offering this incident in the life of a certain monk: Externally his religious observance was the same as that of the other monks, but he had attained such sanctity that the mere touch of his garments healed the sick. Marveling at these deeds, since his life was no more exemplary than the life of the other monks, the superior asked him one day what was the cause of these miracles.

He replied that he too was mystified and was at a loss as to how to account for such happenings. "What devotions do you practice?" asked the abbot. He answered that there was little or nothing special that he did beyond making a great deal of willing only what God willed, and that God had given him the grace of abandoning his will totally to the will of God.

"Prosperity does not lift me up, nor adversity cast me down," added the monk. "I direct all my prayers to the end that God's will may be done fully in me and by me." "That raid that our enemies made against the monastery the other day, in which our stores were plundered, our granaries put to the torch and our cattle driven off — did not this misfortune cause you any resentment?" queried the abbot.

"No, Father," came the reply. "On the contary, I returned thanks to God — as is my custom in such circumstances — fully persuaded that God does all things, or permits all that happens, for his glory and for our greater good; thus I am always at peace, no matter what happens." Seeing such uniformity with the will of God, the abbot no longer wondered why the monk worked so many miracles.[11]

Alphonsus considers that everything that happens is for the best.

God wills only our good; God loves us more than anybody else can or does love us.... Even chastisements come to us, not to crush us, but to make us mend our ways and save our souls: *"Let us believe that these scourges of the Lord have happened for our amendment and not for our destruction"* (Jdt 8:27).[12]

When persons make God's will their own, God frequently does what they want. "Indeed," says Alphonsus, "what can be more satisfactory to a person than to experience the fulfillment of all his desires? This is the happy lot of the man who wills only what God wills...."[13]

Alphonsus observes that a person who does God's will is always consistent:

> The Holy Spirit warns us: *"Do not winnow with every wind"* (Si 5:11), that is: "Do not be swayed by every wind that blows." Some people resemble weather vanes that turn about according to which way the wind blows. If the wind is favorable to their desires, you see them cheerful and good-natured; but if there is a contrary wind and things do not turn out as they wish, you see them sad and impatient. And so they do not become saints and they lead an unhappy life....[14]

Alphonsus assures us that the fruit of uniformity with God's will is a foretaste of heaven.

> By uniting themselves to the divine will, the saints have enjoyed paradise by anticipation in this life.... St. Mary Magdalene of Pazzi derived such consolation at hearing the words "will of God," that she usually fell into an ecstasy of love.[15]

Like the other saints, Alphonsus invites us to pray in order that we may accomplish God's will:

> When anything disagreeable happens, remember it comes from God and say at once, "This comes from God" and be at peace.... Form the habit of offering yourself frequently to God by saying, "My God, behold me in your presence; do with me and all that I have as you please." This was the constant practice of St. Teresa. At least fifty times a day she offered herself to God, placing herself at his entire disposition and good pleasure.[16]

75

St. Mary Magdalene of Pazzi used to say that all our prayers should have no other purpose than that of obtaining from God the grace to follow his holy will in all things.[17]

He then explains in great detail those matters in which we should unite ourselves to God's will:

In external matters. In times of great heat, cold or rain; in times of famine, epidemics and similar occasions we should refrain from expressions like these: "What unbearable heat!" "What piercing cold!" "What a tragedy!" In these instances we should avoid expressions indicating opposition to God's will....

In personal matters. In matters that affect us personally, let us acquiesce in God's will. For example, in hunger, thirst, poverty, desolation, loss of reputation....

Let us not lament if we suffer from some *natural defect* of body or mind; from poor memory, slowness of understanding, little ability...or general bad health....

Who knows? Perhaps if God had given us greater talent, better health, a more personable appearance, we might have lost our souls!

It is especially necessary that we be resigned in *corporal infirmities....* We ought to make use of the ordinary remedies...but if they are not effective, let us unite ourselves to God's will and this will be better for us than would be our restoration to health.... Certainly, it is more virtuous not to complain in times of painful illness; still and all, when our sufferings are excessive, it is not wrong to let our friends know what we are enduring, and also to ask God to free us from our sufferings.... We have the example of our Lord, who, at the approach of his bitter passion, made known his state of soul to his disciples, saying: *"My soul is sorrowful even unto death"* (Mt 26:38) and besought his eternal Father to deliver him from it.... But our Lord likewise taught us what we should do when we have made such a petition, when he added: *"Nevertheless, not as I will, but as you will"* (Mt 26:39).[18]

The time of spiritual desolation is also a time for being resigned. When a soul begins to cultivate the spiritual life, God usually showers his consolations upon it...but when he sees it making solid progress, he withdraws his hand to test its love.... I do not say you will feel no pain in seeing yourself deprived of the sensible presence of God; it is impossible for the soul not to feel it and lament over it, when even our Lord cried out on the cross: *"My God, my God, why have you forsaken me?"* (Mt 27:46). In its sufferings, however, the soul should always be resigned to God's will.[19]

Finally, we should be united to God's will in regard to the *time* and *manner* of our death. One day St. Gertrude, while climbing up a small hill, lost her footing and fell into a ravine below. After her companions had come to her assistance, they asked her if while falling she had any fear of dying without the sacraments. "I earnestly hope and desire to have the benefit of the sacraments when death is at hand," she replied; "still, to my way of thinking, the will of God is more important."[20]

Lastly, we should unite ourselves to the will of God as regards our *degree* of grace and glory.... We should desire to love God more than the seraphim, but not to a degree higher than God has destined for us.[21]

Last but not least, Alphonsus stresses the importance of doing God's will as it is expressed for us by our superiors:

St. Vincent de Paul used to say, "God is more pleased by the sacrifice we offer him when we subject our will to obedience, than by all the other sacrifices we can offer him; because in giving him other things...we give him things we possess, but in giving him our will we give him ourselves."[22]

PART II
THE WORD OF LIFE

THE WORD OF LIFE
AND THE FATHERS OF THE CHURCH

Let us draw closer to that treasure which has accompanied our life now for many years. I mean the Word of Life, the word of God.

But what is the word of God?

I remember one day the answer became very clear to me when I read in the Gospel: "These men you gave me were yours; they have kept your word. Now they realize that all you gave me comes from you. I entrusted to them the message you entrusted to me, and they received it. They have known that in truth I came from you, they have believed it was you who sent me" (Jn 17:6-8).

In reading this passage I had the impression in the depths of my soul that the phrases "your word," "all you gave me," "the message you entrusted to me," and "I came from you"—that all these phrases were somehow synonymous, that is, that the words pronounced by Jesus were Jesus himself, the Word pronounced from eternity by the Father.

It seemed to me, therefore, that this was an exciting discovery, and I wanted to see it confirmed in St. Augustine's commentary on the same passage. Here it is: "Everything the Father has given to the Son, he has given it in generating him. . . . In what other way would he give some words to the Word, since in the Word he has said everything in an ineffable way?"[1] Thus, we were in agreement with St. Augustine.

But let us proceed in order.

The Word of Life, like all the fundamental aspects of our spiritual ideal life, has a story behind it.

When I was a student, I was hungry for truth; for that reason I was studying philosophy. More than that, like many other young people, I was seeking truth and I thought I could find it through study. But here is one of the key ideas dating from the very first days of the Focolare, and I immediately shared it with my companions: Why must we go looking for the truth when the truth lives embodied in Jesus, the God-man?

If the truth draws us, let us leave everything, let us seek him and follow him.

And this is what we have done.

We have taken the Gospel and we have read it word by word. And we have found it all new. We found light bursting out from every part of it. In fact, every word of Jesus was like a beam of brilliant light: totally divine!

That seemed to be the answer to my previous searching.

The Gospel could be compared to no other book, because in the Gospel it is God himself who speaks. "The One who comes from above is above all," says St. John, "the one who is of the earth is earthly, and he speaks on an earthly plane" (Jn 3:31).

This is the difference between what we say and what Jesus says: he comes from above; we come from the earth.

His words are unique, eternal: "Though the grass withers and the flower wilts, the word of our God stands forever" (Is 40:8).

These words struck us as spellbinding, written with the divine touch. They possessed a tremendous majesty.[2] They were words of life to be translated into life, words which were universal in both space and time.

Jesus in fact is risen. He lives in the present. This must be our conviction as it was in the primitive Church.

And if Jesus is risen and lives, his words—even though pronounced in the past—are not simply records of the past, but words he is addressing today to all of us and to people of every age of time.

The words of Jesus!

They must have been his greatest art, if we may say that. The Word, who speaks in human words: what content, what intensity, what a force, what a voice!

In comparison with the Gospel, everything which was not inspired by God seemed to be watered down, even though it dealt with spiritual topics; and the theories of the great thinkers, even though at times they revealed some partial truth, seemed to dissolve into thin air.

The experience of certain Fathers of the Church was renewed in us. Listen to what St. Gregory Nazianzen says: "The great word of God throws into darkness all the many discourses produced by the human spirit; no matter how good and convincing they may be, as the sun at its zenith overcomes every other splendor."[3]

And St. Basil: "...One day arising as from a deep sleep I looked out upon the marvelous light of the truth of the Gospel, and beheld the uselessness of the wisdom 'of the rulers of this age, who are men headed for destruction' (1 Cor 2:6)."[4]

And St. Justin the philosopher affirmed:

> Everything that the philosophers and legislators uncovered and expressed well, they accomplished through their discovery and contemplation of some part of the Word. But, since they did not have a full knowledge of the Word, which is Christ, they often contradicted themselves.[5]

And elsewhere he concluded: "While pondering Christ's words, I discovered that his was the only sure and useful philosophy."[6]

St. Thérèse of Lisieux, like ourselves, found the words of human beings barren in comparison with those of God. This is the source of her love for the Gospel:

> I've only to open a spiritual book — even the finest, even the most affecting of them — to find my heart shut up against it; I can't think about what I'm reading, or else it just gets as far as my brain without helping me to meditate at all. I can only escape from this inhibition of mine by reading Holy Scripture.... Above all it's the Gospels that occupy my mind when I'm at prayer; my soul has so many needs, and yet this is the one thing needful. I'm always finding fresh lights there; hidden meanings which had meant nothing to me hitherto.[7]

St. Teresa of Avila writes: "I have always been fond of the words of the Gospels and I have found more recollection in them than in the most carefully planned books — especially books of which the authors were not fully approved, and which I never wanted to read."[8]

We have come into contact with the word of God in many different ways — in the liturgy, in meditation, and so on. Two ways have characterized our beginnings: to listen to the word of God within us — as we used to say to listen to "that little voice" — and to put into practice one word of God, usually one taken from the Gospel, for a certain period of time.

We used to look with admiration in fact upon the group that St. Augustine formed with his disciples and we used to repeat one of his sayings, "The truth dwells within us."

Since the first Focolarine* were Christians, the word of God was a reality which had been put into their hearts from the

---

*Members of focolare centers, small communities of either men or women, whose first aim is to achieve among themselves the unity Jesus prayed for.

time they were children when they first came to know Christianity. Gradually the action of the Holy Spirit had made them always more aware of this. Thus, it was common to hear this mutual encouragement: "listen to that voice," especially as a form of advice at the moment for making a decision. John says, in fact, "The word of God remains in you" (1 Jn 2:14) and speaks of "the truth that abides in us and will be with us forever" (2 Jn 2).

The Holy Spirit was urging us not to overlook that source of truth that was already springing from the inner depths of our souls.

The second way that the Lord had indicated for us to assimilate the Gospel was that of *living the word.*

We would take into consideration one complete sentence of the Scriptures; we would meditate on it; we would make a commentary which we wanted to be confirmed by those who represented the Church for us. Then we would live it.

The Lord — as we understood much later — was putting into our hands the alphabet, so that we would get to know Christ. We need to know just a few letters and just a few grammar rules — we would say — and then we know how to write and to read. But if we don't know them we remain illiterate for the rest of our lives. A few sentences of the Gospel were enough to form Christ in us.

This idea of the alphabet is not new. I have discovered that others have used it; and this makes us feel that we are children of just one mother, the Church, and brothers and sisters of the saints.

St. Bonaventure teaches that "the disciples of Christ must study the Holy Scriptures like children who learn how to say 'A, B, C,' and then learn how to make syllables, and then learn how to read, and later on to form sentences."[9]

And St. Gertrude, a great saint, says:

Put before me your marvelous alphabet.... Teach me to experience the glorious A of your beautiful love. Do not hide from me the fruitful B of your royal wisdom. Show me accurately the individual letters of your charity, so that with the eyes of my heart, which have been purified by truth, I may penetrate into the most hidden parts of your delight and may behold, study, learn, know, and recognize, as much as is possible in this life, the characters of this heavenly alphabet.[10]

We were living the word of God. *Living* it: this is what the Holy Spirit was mostly urging us to do. It was an inner voice that was re-echoing what had already been written: "Act on this word. If all you do is listen to it, you are deceiving yourselves" (Jm 1:22). And "anyone who hears my words and puts them into practice is like the wise man who built his house on rock" (Mt 7:24).

This is what the saints have done. St. Hilary says: "There is no word of God that should not be fulfilled; and everything that has been said carries within itself the need to be put into practice. The words of God are decrees."[11]

But we were not living the word of God individually, each of us on our own. The useful experiences, the insights, and the graces received through living the word, were put in common and had to be shared in common, because one of the demands of our spirituality is that we are to make progress in sanctity together. As a result, those who listened were blessed and those who spoke were enriched.

In fact, says St. Maximus: "The nature of the spiritual word is such that when its effect follows, a mutual benefit results, refreshing both those who listen and those who speak."[12]

And St. Bernard also says:

In you, my brothers,...I do indeed find "ears to hear"...and sometimes even during my sermon it seems to me that I can actually feel the burning fervor of your hearts. For the more plentifully you suck out the milk of the word, the more abundantly does the Holy Spirit replenish my breasts...and the more copious is the supply given me for your nourishment.[13]

We felt we had a duty to share with others what we were experiencing also because we realized that whenever we would give, the experience remained and served to build up our own interior life, while if we failed to give, little by little our souls were impoverished.

Therefore, we lived the word with intensity throughout the whole day. And then the fruits would be communicated not only among ourselves but also with the people who were becoming part of the initial group. It was like a password and everyone wanted to take hold of it in order to have the certainty of being included in the newborn community.

What was being born from this was really something new. To understand this well we must bear in mind that before this happy moment, a moment of special enlightenment by the Holy Spirit about the word of God, we were not used to living the word of God like this, that is, to applying it to all the circumstances of our lives and to sharing the effects with one another.

At most we used to meditate on the word of God, penetrate it with our mind, see if we could derive some thoughts from it, and, if we were fervent, make some resolutions.

But here was something utterly different. Now the Word of Life was examined for its most varied applications through continual contact with life and it began to achieve a transformation of each individual and of the group. When we were living it, it was no longer the "I" or "we" who lived, but the word in me, the word in the group. And this was a Christian revolution with all its consequences.

We could see clearly that the word had been the seed of a tree blossoming in each one of us and in the heart of the community.

And Jesus spoke about seed in the parable of the sower, when he explained how the word is sown in different soils and with different results.

This reality of the seed, so alive ever since the first moments of the Focolare, calls to mind Isaiah:

> For just as from the heavens the rain and snow come down and do not return there till they have watered the earth, making it fertile and fruitful, giving seed to him who sows and bread to him who eats, so shall my word be that goes forth from my mouth; it shall not return to me void, but shall do my will, achieving the end for which I sent it. (Is 55:10-11)

I remember that the outsiders who were observing this phenomenon were surprised to find a living Christian community rather than merely a word of the Gospel being meditated upon. And they sometimes wondered what strange meditations these might be which we had on the word of God.

The fact is that the very destiny of the seed is to die in order to give life to the tree, just as the destiny of the word of God is to be "eaten" in order to give life to Christ in us and to Christ among us. St. Jerome gives magnificent expression to this marvelous development:

> The preaching of the Gospel is the smallest among all the philosophical doctrines. When we announce the scandal of the Cross, there is no other truth than the faith in the death of our Lord Jesus Christ. Now try to compare this teaching to the systems of the philosophers, to their books, to the splendor of their eloquence, and you will see how the Gospel is the smallest among all the other seeds. But those doctrines, when they develop, show nothing which is alive, concrete, vital, but they all wither and dry up, and rot. On the contrary, this preaching, which seemed so small at the beginning, when it has grown in the souls of believers all over the world, doesn't become like grass, but grows like a tree.[14]

ALWAYS BE THE WORD

In the beginning was the Word;
the Word was in God's presence,
and the Word was God.
He was present to God in the beginning.
Through Him all things came into being....
(Jn 1:1-3)

The Word, who is God, came one day among us, fulfilled his mission as Redeemer, and then ascended to heaven, to his Father's side.

But his real presence has remained, in different ways, all over the earth: in the Eucharist, in his word, in our midst when we are united in his name, within each one of us, and in the hierarchy of the Church.

One of the real presences of the Word, who is God, is therefore the word of God.

"I want to speak to you about the word of God," says St. Augustine. "What is this word? What is its greatness? 'Through it all things came into being.' Look at the works and be struck with awe before the one who did those works. 'Through the Word all things came into being'!"[1]

Augustine saw clearly the activity of the Word in the act of creation, and therefore its divine omnipotence, its dizzying height. The Word of God!

There are many things which God willed should be proclaimed and made known by his servants the Prophets, but how much more important are those which his Son speaks, which the Word of God who was in the Prophets testifies with his own voice.[2]

And his words cannot be other than "spirit and life." Through them we pass from death to life; and by giving life to all things they penetrate everything. "Indeed, God's word is living and effective," says St. Paul, "sharper than any two-edged sword. It penetrates and divides soul and spirit...it judges the reflections and thoughts of the heart" (Heb 4:12).

But if God's word is the Word of God, it would have been logical, at the beginning of the Focolare and at every moment, for talks containing the word to have had extraordinary effects on the people who heard them: they should have been radiant with such splendor and such majesty that many would be convinced and strongly impelled to lead a good life.

And so it would have been logical that those who professed themselves obedient to religion would be surrounded by great esteem and veneration.

The fact is that not infrequently we experienced great sorrow in hearing disparaging remarks about what should have been an echo of the words of Jesus, a spark of supernatural light, an anointing of the Spirit: preaching the word. At times sermons became synonymous with empty lectures, boring and barren of impact.

We noticed likewise that many religious people brought upon themselves the contempt and hatred of the world, not because they were living the Gospel, but rather because by the inconsistency of their lives they were emptying the Gospel of its content.

This fact made us blush because up to that moment we ourselves were certainly identified with those Christians. This realization branded an indelible convinction upon our hearts: it is necessary first to live and then to speak. This is how Jesus had acted: he began to do and then to teach (cf. Ac 1:1).

This same pattern — besides being in Scripture — can be seen also in the Fathers of the Church.

St. John Chrysostom affirmed:

> ...Jesus says that first we must act and then we can teach others how to act. He put the practice of what is good before the teaching of it, showing that we can usefully teach only after having put into practice whatever is being taught, and never any other way.
>
> Elsewhere Jesus says: "Physician, heal yourself" (Lk 4:23). The one who is incapable of putting his own life in order and attempts to instruct others, runs the risk of being ridiculed by many; or rather, he will not even be able to teach, because his actions will bear witness to the very opposite of his words.[3]

The proclamation of the word without the testimony of deeds was a scandal to the pagans as it is today to non-Christians, and it leads to reproach, as formerly it used to lead to blasphemy rather than conversion.

In the second letter of St. Clement of Rome to the Corinthians, we read:

> When the pagans hear from our lips the oracles of God, they marvel at their beauty and greatness. But then when they observe that our actions are unworthy of the words we utter, they turn to blasphemy, saying that it is a myth and a deception.[4]

And again St. Augustine:

> His words remain in us when we do what he has commanded us and we desire what he has promised us; but when, on the contrary, his words remain only in our memory, but leave not a trace in our life and our behavior, then the branch is no longer part of the vine, because it no longer drinks in life from its roots.[5]

91

And the conviction that it was necessary first to live and then to speak was so strong among us that we were not content to live the word only when the occasion presented itself, but we nourished ourselves with the word every instant of our lives. We discovered that just as the body breathes in order to live, so the soul in order to keep alive must live the word.

And this manner of living the word has remained the secret of our renewal and of our Christian revolution.

I have the impression that if every day we were to repeat to ourselves, and to all who live with us, the idea of putting the word into practice, we would have rendered one of the greatest services to the cause of Jesus.

"Let our mind," says St. Ambrose, "remain *always* with him; let it never leave his temple, let it never be separated from his word. Let us remain ever intent upon the reading of Scripture, upon meditation, upon prayer, so that the word of 'Him who is' may be ever at work in us."[6]

When we read certain writings from the first years of the Focolare, we notice a remarkable thrust of the Spirit in this direction.

Here is a letter I wrote in 1948:

> We have understood that the world needs a treatment of...the Gospel, because only the Good News can give back to the world the life it lacks. This is why we live the Word of Life....
>
> We *make it flesh* in ourselves to the point of being that living word....
>
> One word would be enough to make one a saint, to make a person another Jesus.
>
> With the passage of time we live many words of Sacred Scripture, so that these stay with us as permanent treasures in our souls.
>
> To live the word in the present moment of our lives—this is our talk.
>
> And all of us can live it, whatever our vocation, whatever

our age, our gender, our social situation, because Jesus is Light for every person who comes into this world.

With this simple method we re-evangelize our souls and with them the world....

Try to live it and you will find all of perfection and, just as every morning you are content with that Sacred Host which you receive, without desiring some other one, in the same way be satisfied with this Word. And you will find in it, as St. Francis used to find in it, "the hidden manna of a thousand fragrances."

In this way and only in this way: in doing the truth, we love! Otherwise, love is empty sentimentalism. For real love is Christ Jesus, is the Truth, the Gospel!

Let us be living Gospels, living words of life, another Jesus! And then we will really love him, and we will imitate Mary, the Mother of the Light, of the Word: the living word.

We have no other book except the Gospel; we have no other science, no other art.

There is Life!

He who finds it does not die.

And now we wish that, as the Focolare grows more and more widespread, it will always be possible to say of us: "...Let what you heard from the beginning remain in your hearts. If what you heard from the beginning does remain in your hearts, then you in turn will remain in the Son and in the Father" (1 Jn 2:24).

And from the beginning there have been three daily communions for the members of the Focolare: communion with Jesus in the Eucharist, with the Word of Life, and with our neighbors.

And the love for the word was so constant and important that it made us say that the uniform of the Focolarino is the word of God.

In 1950, I wrote this:

> ...For us, for each of us, the Word of Life is the gown, the wedding garment of our soul which is the bride of Christ. And this is for us what the habit is for religious orders. They who are members of religious congregations sanctify themselves only insofar as they remain in their vocation. They cannot change it. They cannot change the habit that they wear. For us the habit is totally interior....

Furthermore the Lord showed us Mary, the Christian *par excellence,* wholly clothed in the word of God, or better, she was the word of God personified.

We saw this, to be the word of God, as the very essence, the very being of every member of the Movement.

This is why we laid such stress upon communion with the word of God as well as communion with the Eucharist and of course with our neighbors, because it was our custom to share every day the experience of the Word of Life with our brothers and sisters.

The Fathers, who reflect the mentality of the primitive Church, often put the word and the Eucharist on the same level.

St. Clement of Alexandria indicates that we must be nourished with the seed of life contained in the Bible the same way we nourish ouselves with the Eucharist.[7]

"My refuge is the Gospel, which is for me like the flesh of Jesus," says St. Ignatius of Antioch.[8]

And St. Jerome: "We eat his flesh and drink his blood in the divine Eucharist, but also in the reading of the Scripture."[9]

St. Gregory Nazianzen compares the reading of Scripture to the eating of the Paschal Lamb.

And Tertullian, in his book *On the Resurrection* makes a

comparison between the life-giving word and the flesh of the Son of God.

And the wise Origen writes that the words which nourish the soul are, in a way, another body with which the Son of God has clothed Himself.

And St. Augustine says this in one of his sermons:

> Tell me, my brothers, which is of greater worth, the word of God or the body of Christ? If you want your answer to be truthful, you must agree with me that the word is not less than the Body of Christ. Now when the Body of Christ is given us, we take great care that no particle of it falls to the ground. In the same way we must be careful that the word of God, when it is given to us, should not vanish from our hearts because we think or speak of other things. The one who hears the word of God negligently will be no less guilty than the one who, out of distraction, lets the Body of Christ fall to the ground.[10]

To conclude this comparison between the word of God and the Eucharist, I will refer to what Vatican II says:

> The Church has always venerated the divine Scriptures just as she venerates the body of the Lord, since from the table of both the word of God and of the body of Christ she unceasingly receives and offers to the faithful the bread of life, especially in the sacred liturgy.[11]

Nothing remains but to set forth along this way strongly attached to the word. The word, like the Eucharist, has multiplied the presence of Jesus on the earth.

This is a great comfort to us, but at the same time it is a great responsibility if we want to present ourselves to the world as authentic followers of Jesus.

What could be greater? What could be more magnificent?

THE EFFECTS OF THE WORD

If we observe people who live the word of God, we notice a great variety of effects which the word works in them. Every soul is like a crystal with many different facets and as the light of the word touches the different facets, it reveals different nuances of color. The situations in which people can find themselves are infinite, and infinite are the reactions which the word, the word of God, can work in each person.

If we had to list the fruits which the word can generate, they would be very many. Thus, we will mention only a few of them.

The word makes us live

Whoever is in contact with an environment of the Focolare where the word of God is lived, has the strong impression in his or her soul that there is "life." And a person can see this from many things: from the expressions of those who welcome their guest, from their gestures, from their readiness to serve, and from a certain youthfulness not only in their souls but also in their bodies. This is so because the word is "life."

St. Athanasius, commenting on this sentence of the Psalm, "Your saying makes me live," says this: "There is nothing which makes the rational soul live its specific life like the word of God."[1]

The word makes us free

This is another characteristic of the word of God, for, as the Gospel says, "The truth will make you free" (Jn 8:32). The truth makes us free because if we place the word above all our thoughts, above all our feelings, above our will, everything else becomes secondary, whatever happens to us. It is secondary whether we are unfortunate or fortunate, whether we experience tragedies or romantic adventures, whether we are sick or healthy — everything is secondary.

What is valuable for us is that throughout all these things we have lived the word.

If we have done that, then we feel we possess a great freedom — freedom from people; freedom from circumstances, whether sad or joyful; freedom from ourselves; freedom from the world which tries to destroy in every possible way the peace of the kingdom of God within us.

The word guarantees happiness

Pope Paul VI says: "The Gospel is a guarantee of happiness...but it changes the nature of happiness. It does not consist in anything ephemeral, but it consists in possessing the Kingdom of God, in the vital communication with Him."[2]

One experiences this happiness as something serene as a sunrise, fresh, sweet, and complete, something that makes our souls leap and want to break into song with a *Te Deum* and a *Magnificat* at the same time. It is unique. It cannot be confused with anything else. Those who have this experience think of it at different moments of their lives because it is a white and luminous mountain peak that they recall as a little Tabor of their souls.

The word converts

Getting to know the Focolare and being converted usually happen together. As a result, we have witnessed wonderful things happen.

We see people who were attached to themselves, to the world, and to their own careers—we see them seek the last place. We see others who could not speak even in front of a small group of people become capable of speaking about their new discovery to crowds. Also our experience has been that those who suffer temptations against chastity feel relieved and transformed by living this ideal. Moreover, especially during the first months, their temptations seem to disappear. And we have noticed that usually the money which is given to the poor or for the works of the Focolare is often given by those who have worked very hard to get it and to save it. We find other people who have become very zealous in the work of God after having been discouraged and hopeless for years; now they say they have "made a discovery." Finally, we have noted how the love which is at the heart of our spirituality can restrain angry people to such a degree that we might never know during the rest of their lives that anger was their chief defect.

We might mention many other effects of living the word. For example, St. Gregory the Great says:

> Through the strength of the divine word the proud one finds humility, the shy one trust, those who live in lust become free in chastity, and those who are greedy find a new balance so that they are restrained in their ambition, and the discouraged one finds new life in the righteousness of zeal, and those who are angry and impulsive find new control. This is the way that God irrigates all things with his waters. He adapts the strength of his word to individuals according to the differences in their behavior, so that each one may find in his word what he needs to bring about the indispensable seed of virtue.[3]

The word purifies us

We have the impression that when we have placed all of our past in the hands of God's mercy and have begun to live the word again, then the word has purified everything in us. And this is very true! "You are clean already," says the Lord, "thanks to the word I have spoken to you [and you have put into practice]" (Jn 15:3).

St. Ambrose has written: "These are words, it is true; but they cleanse us."[4]

The word draws us to our specific vocation

Now when the word is lived, it raises up in the midst of the community the most varied callings. Some are called to virginity, some to the priesthood, some to religious life, some to a marriage that is truly a Christian community, a "little church," because it reflects the life of the whole Church, and some to a lay life that remains immersed in the world, with all its complications and involvements, and yet wills to make God prevail over all other ideals.

The word brings forth the hatred of the world and the sanctity of the disciple

When the word is lived by the disciples of Jesus, those who observe them from the outside do not remain indifferent. It is not rare for this new life to arouse implacable criticism. I would say, moreover, that if the world does not rebel against the evangelical life, then the disciples of Jesus, who are supposed to be at odds with the world, cannot be called those who "are not of the world." At times this criticism reaches the point of hatred, and so we see the great martyrs of the Church. We also find other martyrs, sometimes among members of the Focolare too that are hurt and at times over-come by a lack of understanding from those who ought to understand them most of all.

At the same time that the evangelical life produces misunderstanding and hatred, it is also the way that leads to sanctity.

We cannot speak of persons still living, but we can affirm with certainty that not a few members of the Focolare who have now passed to the next life, may be considered as little saints. We can see this from the ways in which they met very difficult situations and very painful illnesses, and from the conversions which took place around their beds just when they approached the next life. Their own deaths gave witness to it, and even their funerals, which were often surrounded by an atmosphere of paradise. In fact, on returning home, those who participated in them said that they seemed to be participating at a wedding feast.

With the Curé of Ars we repeat: In my cemetery — and ours is as large as the world — saints are sleeping.

We have, therefore, hatred and sanctity — two classical effects of those who live the word. But Jesus himself affirms it: "I gave them your word, and the world has *hated* them for it; they do not belong to the world, any more than I belong to the world.... Sanctify them by means of truth — your word is truth" (Jn 17:14,17).

The word makes us see the truth

At times when we talk with children and with young people who are living the word, we feel like saying: the Spirit is speaking in you. The reason is that they give us the impression that they "see" in a special way.

How true are the words of St. Augustine: "Now you are believers, if you persevere in your faith, you will see... and you will come to know the truth."[5]

The word brings comfort

How many times the saints, and we Christians also, when caught in the grip of a doubt, or a decision that must be made, or a misfortune which befalls us, take the Bible and open it to find comfort. Let us repeat what is written in the book of Maccabees: "We have for our encouragement the sacred books that are in our possession" (1 M 12:9).

The word gives us joy

Above all, the word of God is a bearer of joy. All the manifestations of the Focolare are characterized by joy.

St. Ambrose says that a person "well instructed and intent upon the word of God will do nothing unreasonable which could cause him to be sad, but rather, always master of his own actions, he will know how to preserve unchanged the joy of a clear conscience."[6]

The word produces works

The word of God bears abundant fruit and its works flourish luxuriantly. For many years we have been spectators of this more than actors, beholding the various works produced through the members of the Focolare. It has been such a spontaneous and continuous growth that of itself it bears witness to the work of God.

St. John Damascene says: "Like a tree planted by a stream of water, so also the soul, watered by the divine Scriptures, grows and prospers...and is always adorned with green leaves, works, that is, which are beautiful in the eyes of God."[7]

The word gives wisdom

The word of God is wisdom. And wisdom is light for every situation: when there is a need to clarify some doubt, to proclaim justice or to know how to rule well, or to be enlightened concerning God's plans for individuals or for the world.

St. Paul tells Timothy: "You, for your part, must remain faithful to what you have learned and believed, because you know who your teachers were. Likewise, from your infancy you have known the sacred Scriptures, the source of wisdom. . . .

"All Scripture," continues St. Paul, "is useful for teaching — for reproof, correction, and training in holiness, so that the man of God may be fully competent and equipped for every good work" (2 Tm 3:14,16).

The word preserves us from human concerns

We see that while many are caught up in the concerns of this world, whoever lives the word is at peace and is not afraid of anything.

This is confirmed by St. John Chrysostom: "The sea rages but you navigate in tranquillity; at the helm is the reading of Scripture and the temptation of things to be done will not cripple the rudder."[8]

The word obtains everything

By living the word of God we obtain everything.

It is impossible to exaggerate, for I am certain that every single day, all over the world where the word is lived, graces beyond number are received. I say it, for the glory of God, because I could not count all the times this has happened to me also.

This is logical, and Jesus says this himself: "If you live in me, and my words stay part of you, you may ask what you will — it will be done for you" (Jn 15:7).

The word brings about union with God

When people get into the practice of living the word of God, they are aware of this result in their soul: communion with Jesus. There are many manifestations of this, such as the ease with which they converse with Jesus. They call upon him in times of need, they rejoice in his presence in the depths of their souls, and they feel that the interior life has come to birth in them, grafted like branches onto the vine which is Christ.

When the word of God is assimilated inwardly, it places the soul under the action of the Holy Spirit, in a living union with Jesus. This is not a superficial contact or encounter, but a profound communion of life.

The word gives us hope of eternal life

The word has generated, and continues to generate within the Focolare, the conviction that just as we see each day all the promises of the Gospel come true, one by one, so also one day — through the word — the gate of heaven will open for the soul.

Indeed, Jesus says: "I solemnly assure you, if a man is true to my word, he shall never see death" (Jn 8:51).

The word makes us one

The word of God is what bound us together from the very first days when we were all close to one another, and it is what still binds us together even now that we are spread far and wide all over the world. It is a light that the senses cannot grasp and that is unknown to the world, but is more precious to God than anything else. Each of us can be another Jesus: a living word of God.

Here is something I wrote in 1948:

> Let us remain united in the name of Jesus, living the Word of Life which makes us one.
>
> ...I have thought about the engrafting that takes place in plants, when two branches are stripped of their bark and by the contact between the two "living" parts, they become one thing.
>
> When can two souls be truly living in unity? When they are "alive," that is, when they are "stripped" of all that is merely human, when they have lived and incarnated the Word of Life so that they become living words. Two "living words" can be made perfect in unity. If one of these is not *alive,* the other one cannot be united with it.
>
> The more I go on, the more I see the beauty of the Word of Life! The richness of the word. A tiny pill that concentrates in itself everything that Jesus brought upon the earth, that is the Gospel message.

Whoever does not live the word causes division

Those who do not live the word of God, bring a merely human atmosphere wherever they go. They will not bring society together, but instead will become a cause of discord and division.

This is what St. Cyprian feared. In his treatise *De unitate,* he dealt principally with the unity of the Church, but he does not fail to urge us over and over again to live the Gospel. He says it is precisely because the Gospel is not lived that there are schisms in the Church.

105

The word changes one's mentality

What the word of God brings about is a complete change of mentality. It injects the sentiments of Christ into the hearts of everyone: Americans, Europeans, Asians, Australians, Africans. Whatever the circumstances, the word makes every citizen of the world a citizen of heaven, a new person.

St. Paul says, "You must...acquire a fresh, spiritual way of thinking. You must put on that new man" (Ep 4:23-24).

The word makes each soul a heaven

From the earliest days of the Focolare, when we wanted to speak about our soul, or the soul of the neighbor who shared the same ideal, we used the term "heaven" — "the heaven of my soul," "the heaven of your soul."

Now, after such a long time, it seems that we understood a deep truth by this use of the word "heaven," for Jesus says: "Anyone who loves me will be true to my word, and my Father will love him; we will come to him and make our dwelling place with him."

We will never come to the end. In brief, the life of the word involves the complete re-evangelization of a person's manner of thinking, of willing, of living. Thus, the Gospel, the law of life, is incarnated.

The Gospel is not a book like other books. Wherever it takes root, it gives rise to a Christian revolution, because the Gospel gives the law of life not only for the union of the soul with God, but also for the union of persons with one another, whether they are friends or enemies. The Gospel lays down as one of its demands the unity of all, and the last will of Jesus will be fulfilled at least in that social milieu where there are Christians who live the Word of Life.

And where a single one of them lives, even the desert will bloom.

THE WORD GENERATES CHRIST

Now we may ask ourselves: how were we able to penetrate the word of God, to grasp it so deeply that we saw it in a new way, charged with vital and revolutionary force?

We can now say that it certainly was because of a special grace, a grace which taught us how to have Christ among us and to live deeply in his presence.

This is what the Lord did: using his own method of teaching, he pointed out to us first of all some words which may seem easier. However, he had a very precise reason for choosing such words. In general, these words referred to love: "Love your neighbor as yourself," "Love one another," "Love your enemy," "Love..."—always love.

It was later that we understood the reason for this choice: those who love obtain the light, because the fruit of loving is interior illumination.

And even more, the love that God places in the soul is supernatural; it is the participation of our love in God's own love, and therefore it is reciprocal love by its very nature. Through this mutual love the Lord slowly accustomed us to experience his presence among us. And this presence of his influenced the understanding of his word. He was the teacher who showed us how to understand his words. In other words, this was the kind of explanation made not by a teacher of theology but rather by Christ himself.

St. Anselm says:

> It is one thing to be fluent in speech and even eloquent; it is
> another thing to enter into the veins and the marrow of heav-

enly words and to contemplate with pure heart the heavenly mysteries. No human teaching, no worldly learning will achieve this. It can be given only by the purity of one's mind and the teaching of the Holy Spirit.[1]

And the presence of Jesus in our midst brings his Spirit.

We also remember that one of the first pages of the Gospel which we read was the Priestly Prayer of Jesus at the Last Supper. It was an event of great importance. The memory is still vivid in our minds of how, as we moved from one word to the next, each word seemed more full of light. And now we understand that it was as if someone were telling us: "Look, you must learn many things in school, but the summary of all is this: 'sanctify them in the truth'. . . 'that all may be one'. . . 'you will have the fullness of joy'. . . 'and you will be one as I am one with the Father,' etc." Thus, the Priestly Prayer of Jesus seemed to us to be the synthesis of the Gospel. And we understood it with an awareness that could only be attributed to a special grace. Once we penetrated those words as far as God wanted us to, it became easier for us to understand the rest of the Gospel.

In fact, we often give this example: imagine a large field on which all the words of the Gospel are written; and at the end of the field imagine the Priestly Prayer of Jesus which synthesizes them all. By this prayer the Lord taught us the unity by which all the evangelical truths are linked together. It was as if he perforated the ground to help us penetrate and understand the rest of the Gospel from the inside by grasping each word at its root, in its truest sense.

After five or six years of living many different words of the Gospel, it became clear to us that they were all similar. There was something that they all had in common. I would say that one had as much value as any other because the effects that were brought about by any of these words in the person who lived them, were identical to the effects produced by any of the others. For example, if we had to live the word: "He who hears

108

you, hears me" (Lk 10:16), we did not wait to put it into practice until we came across a bishop or some type of superior. Rather we tried to live it each second of the day by obeying what we had been taught by the priests in catechism, and what we had learned directly from God and then submitted to the Church. In this way, to live this word was equivalent to living all the other words, like those which tell us to do the will of God, or to love God, or to love our neighbor. Everything, therefore, became more simplified.

Having reached this point, it may have seemed superfluous to continue our practice of laying special stress on one word each week. We saw, however, that God works in our souls and sometimes sends such great gifts of light that we seemed to have received a deeper understanding of the whole Gospel. And this can be a common experience if people respond to his grace.

For example, under the influence of these graces you discover in the Gospel that the whole life of Jesus is oriented towards the Father, and you then reread the Gospel with new interest and you also reorient your own life in the direction that Jesus did.

Then you may receive graces that permit darkness and obscurity in your soul, which is like hell. Then you begin to doubt everything. And the "logic" of the Gospel is what you doubt most. You tell yourself—or rather, someone devilish insinuates to you: "if you love you will *see*, and then you will find yourself trapped by the *system*,"—that is, by a supernatural life which, at that point, appears to you as something dangerous that will take away your freedom. Therefore: "Don't move! Don't love, and you will be yourself!" The devil will do everything to keep you from loving. But if you resist and do the exact opposite of what the temptation tells you, a still deeper vision of the Gospel will burst open before the eyes of your soul. And then you rediscover it as the only book of life and you understand that you will never be able to "grasp fully...the breadth and length and height and depth" of the

109

word (Ep 3:18).

In this way, the Gospel remains as the eternal book of your spiritual nourishment.

And now let us go on to another point.

The word of God! The word of God is not like other words. Not only does the word tell us something, but it also has the power of bringing about what it says.

Since the word is Christ, it generates Christ in our souls and in the souls of others.

If we are Christians, then there is grace in us even before we live the word. And with grace we undoubtedly have the light of God and also love, but we are somewhat closed up in a cocoon as a caterpillar. But when we live the Gospel, love radiates light in us and the light makes our love grow: similarly, the pupa in the cocoon starts moving and growing until the butterfly comes out. In the same way, Christ starts to live in us, and then grows more and more...so that we are always open to be more filled with him.

This is what our ideal teaches us. This is what the word of God wants to do in us: to form Christ in us even now, so that our preparation for the next life may be like the apex of a life that was always lived for those days, for that hour, for the true Life.

Popes, saints, fathers...many are those who say that the word generates Christ in us.

Paul VI has given a magnificent description of what the word produces and of the way in which it is to be received. He even suggests a method which we use in the Focolare. The Holy Father says:

> How does Jesus become present in our souls? The divine thought, the Word, the Son of God made Man, comes through this vehicle: the communication of the word. We could assert that the Lord incarnates himself within us when

we allow his word to come and live within us.

When listening to an explanation of the Gospel, every Christian should take special care to choose one key passage as his own. Then, when he returns home, let him nourish himself during the whole of the following week with this nutritious spiritual food: the word of the Lord....

First of all, therefore, to listen, and then...to treasure.... But a passive act of acceptance only is not enough; an active reaction, a reflective act is necessary. One must...meditate.

...And there is a third moment. The word must be placed into action and guide our lives. It must be applied to our style or way of living, of judging, of speaking.

...In such a way, Christian life reveals itself as exceedingly attractive.[2]

And the concept that St. Ignatius of Antioch has of the word is splendid. He feels that since we have come out of the mind of God, we are destined to return there, but as "word of God." When his followers wanted to prevent his martyrdom, he wrote to them: "I would have you think of pleasing God rather than men. If only you will say nothing in my behalf [that is, if you let me go to my martyrdom], I shall be a 'word of God.' "[3]

And St. James the Apostle asserts: "He has generated us of his own will with a word of truth, so that we would be the first among all his creatures" (Jm 1:18).

Then there is another sentence of Jesus in the Gospel that causes us to reflect. When the apostles come to him and tell him that his mother and brothers were waiting for him, Jesus answers: "My mother and my brothers are those who hear the word of God and act upon it" (Lk 8:21). Is there, then, a possibility, acknowledged by Jesus, to be in a certain way "his mother"? Yes, for he said so.

We can generate Christ in souls in the same way that a mother generates, and we can do this precisely through the word.

111

St. Gregory the Great also explains how we can be mothers of Jesus:

> We must know that those who are brothers or sisters of Jesus through faith, become his mothers by means of the word. If, through the word, someone gives birth to love for the Lord in the soul of his neighbor, he virtually *generates the Lord,* because he gives birth to him in the heart of the person who listens to his word, and he becomes mother of the Lord.[4]

In the same way, St. Paul feels very strongly that he has become the father of his followers because he sowed the word in their hearts: "Granted you have ten thousand guardians in Christ but you have only one father. It is I who begot you in Christ Jesus, through my preaching the Gospel" (1 Cor 4:15).

St. Augustine sees the churches as generated by the word of God: "The very Apostles, on whom the Church was founded, following the example of Christ, 'preached the word of truth and generated the Churches.' "[5]

Thus, the Church is generated precisely through the announcing of the word.

And the Church, in turn, is a mother who generates souls through the words she gives and through baptism.

We can say the same thing about the Focolare. It was generated by the words that Jesus sowed in our hearts, and it, in turn, is a mother for many souls because it generates them: it plants the word in the people's hearts and the word is not a mere concept but rather "spirit and life" (Jn 6:63).

The word of God, therefore, *generates Christ* in persons, in communities, and in churches. Because of this, Clement of Alexandria was able to say:

> ...he who obeys the Lord and follows the Scripture which was given to us, is fully transformed into the image of the Master: he comes to live like God in flesh. But this height cannot be

112

reached by those who do not follow God's lead: and he leads through the divinely inspired Scriptures.[6]

To place ourselves in contact with the word of God is, then, to come into vital contact with Christ, to absorb his life. For this reason, echoing The Song of Songs: "Let him kiss me with the kisses of his mouth!" (Sg 1:1), we too can assert: every time that we live the word of Jesus, it is as if we were giving a kiss on his mouth — that mouth that says only words of life. He who is the Word communicates himself to our souls. And we are one with him! Christ is born in us.

St. Gregory of Nyssa expresses the same idea:

> The mouth of the Spouse is a fountain that gives forth the word of eternal life.... It is necessary, then, that those who want to get a drink from the fountain put their mouths next to the water. Now, the fountain is the Lord, who said: "if anyone thirsts, let him come to me; let him drink" (Jn 7:37), and it is because of this that the soul wants to place its mouth next to the mouth from which life springs, saying: "Let him kiss me with kisses of his mouth" (Sg 1:1); and the one who has this fountain for everyone and who wants everyone to be saved, does not allow anyone of those who are saved to be left without this kiss, a kiss which becomes the purification from any stain whatsoever.[7]

After all we have said about the Word of Life, we can draw only one conclusion:

How much longer will we live? Let us live the word in the present moment, each time more and more intensely, so that for the world and for the glory of Christ, we too may be "God in flesh."

PART III
THE EUCHARIST

THE EUCHARIST AND THE
NEW TESTAMENT

For me to talk about you, Jesus in the Eucharist, is really quite daring and presumptuous. For you are present in all the churches of the world, listening to the intimate secrets, the hidden problems, and the sighs of millions of people, seeing the tears of joy in the conversions you alone know about. You are the heart of all hearts, the heart of the Church.

We would prefer not to disturb the silence which is fitting for such a sublime and breathtaking love, except that our own love, eager to overcome every fear, desires to get beyond the veils of the white host and the wine in the golden chalice.

Forgive our daring: for love wants to know better in order to love better. We do not want our journey on earth to be over before we have discovered at least a little about who you are.

Also, since we are Christians, and within our mother the Church we live and spread the ideal of unity, we have to talk about the Eucharist, for none of the mysteries of our faith has so much to do with unity as the Eucharist. The Eucharist opens up unity and reveals its substance. In fact, it is through the Eucharist that a person's unity with God is completely fulfilled, as well as the unity of people among themselves and the unity of the whole cosmos with its Creator.

God became man. Jesus came on earth. It was in his power to do everything and anything. But the logic of love demanded that once he had taken a step like this, that is, to come from the Trinity down to life on earth, he would not stay here for only thirty-three years, although his life on earth was divinely extraordinary. Rather, he had to find a way to remain, and make himself present in every corner of the earth throughout the centuries, and to remain in the culminating moment of his love, the moment of his sacrifice and glory, his death and Resurrection. Indeed, he has remained here. For with divine imagination, he invented the Eucharist. This shows his love reaching beyond all possible limits. St. Thérèse of Lisieux put it this way: "O Jesus, permit me to say, brimming over with gratitude, that your love goes so far as to become madness."[1]

Institution of the Eucharist

Let's see how the event is related to Matthew, Mark, Luke, and Paul. Luke says:

> When the hour arrived, he took his place at table, and the apostles with him. He said to them: "I have greatly desired to eat this Passover with you before I suffer. I tell you, I will not eat again until it is fulfilled in the kingdom of God...." Then, taking bread and giving thanks, he broke it and gave it to them, saying: "This is my body to be given for you; Do this as a remembrance of me." He did the same with the cup after eating, saying as he did so: "This cup is the new covenant in my blood, which will be shed for you." (Lk 22:14-20)

It is only because he is God, that Jesus could unveil realities which were so new, so unforeseeable, so unfathomable, using so few solemn words. These realities could send us into ecstasy because, if we understood them even a little, our human nature could not stand up in front of them.

Jesus was the only one who knew everything, the only one who was aware that his gesture was bringing centuries of expectation to an end, the only one who could look into the infinite consequences of what he was, i.e., the fulfillment of a divine plan which had always been foreseen by the Trinity, the foundation of the Church. It is a plan which starts on earth but penetrates into the mysteries of the kingdom. Only God could have spoken and behaved in that way.

However, something of what his most sacred heart felt in that moment shines through those words "I have greatly desired." They express an immense joy. And the words "Before I suffer" express his embrace of the cross and the bond between suffering and joy, because he was about to make his last will and testament, and a will is not valid until after death. He was leaving us an immense inheritance: himself.

St. Peter Julian Eymard says:

> Jesus Christ too wants to leave his own memorial, his own masterpiece, which would render him immortal in the hearts of his people. It will be an undying reminder of his love for humankind. He will be its inventor, its author. He will consecrate it as his testament. And his death will give it life and glory.... This is the divine Eucharist.[2]

Then Jesus "gave thanks." Eucharist means "great thanksgiving" and the most perfect thanksgiving was the one Jesus made to the Father for having watched over humanity and having saved it by intervening in the most extraordinary ways.

Then taking the bread and the cup he said: "This is my body to be given for you. Do this as a remembrance of me.... This cup is the new covenant in my blood which will be shed for you."

This is the Eucharist. It is the great miracle. The Eucharist, in St. Thomas Aquinas' words, is the greatest of the miracles of Jesus Christ.[3] In fact, as Peter Julian Eymard said,

> It is superior to all the others in its object and surpasses all the others in its duration. It is Jesus' permanent incarnation and perpetual sacrifice. It's like the burning bush burning on the altar forever. It is the manna, the true bread of life which comes down daily from heaven.[4]

119

These are, to use Ignatius of Antioch's expression, "mysteries, loudly proclaimed to the world though accomplished in the stillness of God!"[5] And the Second Vatican Council affirms that "the Most Blessed Eucharist contains the Church's entire spiritual wealth, that is, Christ Himself, our Passover and living bread. Through his very flesh, made vital and vitalizing by the Holy Spirit, He offers life to men."[6]

From the Old to the New Testament

Jesus celebrates his Passover as a banquet. In every home, suppertime is the time of the deepest intimacy, brotherhood, and often of friendship and of celebration.

The banquet over which Jesus presides is celebrated as the Passover of the Jews, and as such it contains in synthesis the entire history of the people of Israel. The Last Supper of Jesus is the fulfillment of all God's promises. The "elements" of the new supper are filled with meaning acquired in the Old Testament. Bread was considered a gift of God, indispensable to life; it was a symbol of communion, a reminder of the manna. Wine, called in Genesis the "blood of grapes" (49:11), was offered in sacrifices (Ex 29:40). It was a symbol of the joy of the future messianic times (cf. Jr 31:12). The cup was a sign of participation in that joy and acceptance of afflictions. It was a reminder of the Covenant of Moses (cf. Ex 24:6). Both bread and wine had been promised by Wisdom to her disciples (cf. Pr 9:1-6).[7]

Like the father of a family, Jesus, in his gestures and in the prayer of benediction, repeats the Judaic rite. But this banquet is totally different and new if compared with the Hebrew Passover: the supper of Jesus is celebrated in the context of his Passion and death. In the Eucharist he anticipates, in a symbolic and real way, his redemptive sacrifice. He is both the priest and the victim.

Pope Paul VI expressed himself in this way on Holy Thursday of 1966:

> We cannot forget that his supper...was a commemorative rite; it was the paschal meal which had to be repeated every year in order to transmit to future generations the indelible reminder of the Hebrew people's liberation from slavery in Egypt.... This evening Jesus substitutes the new covenant for the old. "This is my blood," he will say, "of the New Covenant" (Mt 26:28). With these words Jesus joins his own Passover to the ancient, historical, and figurative Passover and makes it succeed it. Jesus' Passover is also historical but it is final, and at the same time an image of another final event: the *Parousia* [the second coming of Jesus].[8]

The words "I will not drink this fruit of the vine from now until the day when I drink it new with you in my Father's reign" (Mt 26:29)—the last phrase was translated by a famous Scripture scholar as "an appointment in Paradise"—give the Eucharist the character of a banquet which will find its completion after our Resurrection. In reference to the New Testament Passover, St. Athanasius writes: "Already here on earth we can participate in the communion with the risen Christ.... We participate, my beloved, not in a temporary feast but in that which is eternal and heavenly, and we do not portray it with images but we realize it in truth."

Indeed, we no longer eat the flesh of a lamb but "we eat the Word of the Father." For Athanasius, to eat the bread and wine changed into the body and blood of Christ is to celebrate the Passover, that is, to relive it. The Eucharist is indeed a sacrament of communion with the paschal Christ, with a Christ who died and is risen, who has passed over (*pasch* =*passage*). He entered into a new phase of his existence, the glorious one at the right hand of the Father. Therefore, receiving Jesus in the Eucharist really means participating—already here on earth—in his life of glory, in his communion with the Father.[10]

The bread of life

John has his own way of speaking about Jesus in the Eucharist. In the sixth chapter of his Gospel, he tells us that Jesus, the day after multiplying the loaves, gave a great discourse in Capernaum which included these words: "You should not be working for perishable food but for food that remains until life eternal, food which the Son of Man will give you" (Jn 6:27). A little later Jesus presents himself as the true bread that came down from heaven, which is to be received in faith. "I myself am the bread of life. No one who comes to me shall ever be hungry. No one who believes in me shall ever thirst" (Jn 6:35).

And he explains how he will be the bread of life: "...the bread I will give is my flesh for the life of the world..." (Jn 6:51 b).

Jesus already sees himself as bread. This, therefore, is the ultimate purpose of his life here on earth: to be bread in order to be eaten, and to be eaten in order to communicate his own life to us.

"This is the bread that comes down from heaven for a man to eat and never die. I myself am the Living Bread come down from heaven. If anyone eats this bread he shall live forever" (Jn 6:50-51a).

How limited are our views compared with those of Jesus. He, who is infinite, who comes from eternity, has protected a people with miracles and graces. He has built his Church, and sets it on its way towards eternity where life will never end.

During this brief existence of ours, we are often short-sighted and at times we worry over trifles. We are blind; yes, blind. We Christians too are often blind. We may live our faith, but without being fully conscious of it. We understand Jesus in some of his words, which give us consolation or some direction, but we do not see the whole Jesus.

"In the beginning was the Word," then came creation, then the incarnation. And then, by means of the Holy Spirit, we have almost a second incarnation in the Eucharist, which serves us as food in this life while on our journey towards the next. Finally, once we are made divine by his person present in his body and blood in the Eucharist, we will reach the kingdom with Jesus.

When we look at reality in this way, everything acquires its true value. Everything is directed towards the future that we shall reach if we try to live the life of the heavenly city even here below as much as possible. We live it if we are careful, in loving God and all of humankind, to have a love similar to Jesus' love. What an adventure life is!

The Pharisees argued with one another, and Jesus replied and explained, and then reaffirmed his words by saying, "He who feeds on my flesh and drinks my blood remains in me and I in him. Just as the Father who has life sent me, and I have life because of the Father, so the man who feeds on me will have life because of me" (Jn 6:56-57).

"He remains in me and I in him." This shows the unity established between Jesus and the human person who feeds on him made bread. What is transmitted is the fullness of life that is in Jesus which comes to him from the Father. In this way, a person becomes immanent in Jesus.

Albert the Great writes,

> [Christ] embraced us with too much love, because he united us to himself so closely that he is within us, and he himself penetrates into our innermost parts. . . .
>
> Divine love produces an ecstasy. It is right to say this of divine love because it brings God into us and us into God. The Greek term *ekstasis,* in fact, means "being outside oneself." [Jesus] says, indeed, "The man who feeds on my flesh and drinks my blood remains in me and I in him" (Jn 6:56). He says, "He remains in me," that is, he dwells outside of himself; and "I remain in him," that is, I dwell outside of myself. . . . This can be done by his charity, which penetrates into

us...and attracts us to him.... It does not just attract us but it takes us into himself, and he penetrates into us to the very marrow of our bones.[11]

In this stupendous chapter of the Gospel of John, Jesus affirms, "The bread I will give is my flesh for the life of the world" (6:51d). And again, "He who feeds on my flesh and drinks my blood has life eternal and I will raise him up on the last day" (6:54).

"For the life of the world." The Eucharist, therefore, serves even in this world for the purpose of giving us life. But what is life? Jesus told us: "I am the life" (Jn 11:25;14:6). This bread nourishes us on him already here below.

"And I will raise him up on the last day." But what is the Resurrection? Jesus told us: "I am the Resurrection" (Jn 11:25). The Eucharist also gives us life for the other world.

He starts in us his own immortal life, that life which is not interrupted by death. Even though our bodies are corruptible, Christ, the life, remains in our souls and in our bodies as the principle of our immortality.

The Resurrection is simply a great mystery for all those who approach it with human reason alone. But there is a way of living which makes the mystery less incomprehensible. When one lives the Gospel seen from the perspective of unity, he or she experiences, for example, that in carrying out the new commandment of Jesus, mutual love leads to a fraternal unity among people that goes beyond natural, human love. This result, this achievement, is an effect of doing God's will. Jesus in fact knew that if we responded to his immense gifts, we would no longer be his servants or friends but his brothers and sisters, and brothers and sisters with one another, because we would all be nourished on the same life, his life.

To indicate this different kind of family, John the Evangelist uses an evocative image: the vine and the branches (15). The same sap, or we could say the same blood, the same life, that is, the same love (which is the love with which the Father loves

124

the Son) is communicated to us (cf. 17:23-26) and circulates between Jesus and us. We become, therefore, one blood and one body with Christ. It is, then, in the truest and supernaturally deepest sense of the word that Jesus after his Resurrection calls his disciples "brothers" (Jn 20:17). The author of the Epistle to the Hebrews confirms that the risen Jesus "is not ashamed to call them brothers" (Heb 2:11).

Now, once this family of the kingdom of heaven had been formed, how could anyone conceive of death as putting an end to such a work of God? No, God could not involve us in such an absurdity and then leave us there. He had to give us a solution, and he gave it by revealing the truth of the resurrection of the flesh. This truth turns out to be no longer a dark mystery of faith for the believer, but a logical consequence of Christian living. It gives us the immense joy of knowing that we will all meet again with Jesus who has united us as brothers and sisters.

The Eucharist in the Acts of the Apostles

In divine revelation we find the Eucharist again mentioned in the Acts of the Apostles. The early Church was very faithful to Jesus in fulfilling the commandment "Do this in remembrance of me." Of the first community in Jerusalem it is said that "They devoted themselves to the apostles' instruction and the communal life, to the breaking of bread and the prayers" (Ac 2:42). And we read about Paul's apostolate: "On the first day of the week when we gathered for the breaking of bread, Paul preached to them. Because he intended to leave the next day, he kept on speaking until midnight.... Afterward Paul...broke bread, and ate. Then he talked for a long while—until his departure at dawn" (Ac 20:7,11).

The Eucharist in the letters of Paul

Also, in his First Letter to the Corinthians, Paul showed how ardent and firm was his faith in the body and blood of Christ, by writing: "Is not the cup of blessing we bless a sharing in the blood of Christ? And is not the bread we break a sharing in the body of Christ?" And he continues by describing the effect that this mysterious bread works in the persons who receive it: "Because the loaf of bread is one we, many though we are, are one body, for we all partake of the one loaf" (1 Cor 10:16-17).

One body! This is the commentary of St. John Chrysostom:

> We are that self-same body. For what is the bread? The Body of Christ. And what do they become who partake of it? The body of Christ: not many bodies, but one body. For as the bread consisting of many grains is made one so that the grains nowhere appear, so are we conjoined both with each other and with Christ.[12]

Jesus, you have a great plan for us, and you are fulfilling it in the course of the centuries. You want to make us one with you so that we may be where you are. After you came from the Trinity down to earth, it was the will of the Father that you return. However, you did not want to return alone, but together with us. This, then, is the long journey: from the Trinity back to the Trinity, passing through the mysteries of life and death, of suffering and glory.

Fortunately, the Eucharist is also a thanksgiving. Only through the Eucharist can we ever thank you enough.

THE CELEBRATION OF THE EUCHARIST
IN THE LIFE OF THE CHURCH

The history of how the Eucharist has been understood down through the centuries is marked by a deepening awareness of it as, above all others, "the mystery of our faith."

Everything has contributed to unveil the infinite wealth which it contains. Every happy or sad occurrence, the Ecumenical Councils, the ever-watchful and infallible magisterium of the Church, the vital experiences of the saints, the heresies, the wars, the bitter negations, all contributed in God's plan to open the eyes of the faithful to ever new aspects of the Eucharistic mystery. As St. Catherine of Siena says, it is "all God and all man."

God the Son, in his immense love, wished to remain among us. God the Father made all things come together so that Christians would always better understand the Eucharist and what it does for each individual and all humanity. Like the sun which gradually increases the effects of its heat and light until midday, so the understanding of the Eucharist has grown throughout the centuries.

This is no place to dwell on particular historical events, but I will say something in order to praise God. Furthermore, everything concerning the one we love is of immense interest to us.

The celebration of the Eucharist in the early Church

As long as the Church has existed, the Eucharist has always been its heart. We can see that the life of the first generations of the Church revolved around the celebration of the Eucharist. All of its doctrinal and vital aspects were brought into light in the writings of the apostolic fathers and of the apologists, as well as in the acts of the martyrs.

In the year 155, Justin, a martyr described the liturgical celebration as follows:

> On the day which is called Sunday we have a common assembly of all who live in the cities or in the outlying districts, and the memoirs of the Apostles or the writings of the Prophets are read, as long as there is time. Then, when the reader has finished, the president of the assembly verbally admonishes and invites all to imitate such examples of virtue. Then we all stand up together and offer up our prayers.... At the conclusion of the prayers we greet one another with a kiss. Then, bread and a chalice containing wine mixed with water are presented to the one presiding over the brethren. He takes them and offers praise and glory to the Father of all through the name of the Son and of the Holy Spirit, and he recites lengthy prayers and thanksgiving to God in the name of those to whom he granted such favors. At the end of these prayers and thanksgiving, all present express their approval by saying "Amen." ...And when he who presides has celebrated the Eucharist, they whom we call deacons permit each one present to partake of the Eucharistic bread, and wine and water; and they carry it also to the absentees.[1]

And a little further on we find already in Justin an expression of exceptional importance regarding the real presence: "The food which has been made Eucharist by the prayer of his word...is both the flesh and blood of that Jesus who was made flesh."[2]

Furthermore, Justin maintained that objectively the Eucharist is a sacrifice, stressing however that it is a sacrifice of an altogether new type. There is no place any longer for the bloody material sacrifices of the Old Testament. The Eucharist represents the long-awaited spiritual sacrifice since the Word himself is the victim.

The Eucharist also reinforces fraternal charity. Immediately after the distribution of the consecrated elements, wrote Justin:

> The wealthy, if they wish, contribute whatever they desire, and the collection is placed in the custody of the president. [With it] he helps the orphans and widows, those who are needy because of sickness or any other reason, and the captives and strangers in our midst; in short, he takes care of all those in need.[3]

It was already said in the Didache that the Eucharistic bread is a symbol of the unity among the brothers who form the Church: "As this broken bread was scattered upon the mountain tops and after being harvested was made one, so let thy Church be gathered together from the ends of the earth into thy kingdom."[4]

Ignatius of Antioch around the year 100 described the Christian community gathered around the bishop and already structured.

> Let all follow the bishop as Jesus Christ did the Father, and the priests, as you would the Apostles. Reverence the deacons as you would the command of God. Apart from the bishop, let no one perform any of the functions that pertain to the Church. Let that Eucharist be held valid which is offered by the bishop or by one to whom the bishop has committed this charge.[5]

A number of martyrs from the first apostolic communities associated their own sacrifice with the Eucharist. When he was bound to the stake for example, St. Polycarp of Smyrna prayed as follows:

> God...of the whole creation...I bless thee, for having made
> me worthy of this day and hour; I bless thee, because I may
> have a part along with the martyrs, in the chalice of thy Christ,
> unto resurrection in eternal life, resurrection both of soul and
> body in the incorruptibility of the Holy Spirit.[6]

Irenaeus, maintaining that God became a man in order that we might become children of God, considered the Eucharist the cause of the resurrection of the flesh: "Also our bodies, when they receive the Eucharist, are no longer corruptible, having the hope of the resurrection to eternity."[7]

These passages have great value. For the most part they come from the very disciples of the Apostles. The chief points we find in them are: Christ as the center of the community in the celebration of the Eucharist; real communion with the body and the blood of Christ; the Eucharist as a sacrifice; the Christians' awareness of forming one single body through the Eucharist; the sharing of material goods; the crucial importance of unity with the bishop; the bond between one's own sacrifice and that of the Eucharist; and the Eucharist as the cause of our resurrection.

We note also that the liturgical celebration took place in general on "the Lord's day" as a memorial of Christ's Resurrection, and that it was presented at once as a sacred rite even if it preserved a family character. It already followed a definite pattern, though not rigid, made up of readings, prayers, the offering, and consecration of the bread and of the wine mixed with water, and then communion for those present and for absentees.

This format will stay unchanged until the peace of Constantine (313 A.D.) but with a tendency to give an always greater emphasis to the rite itself.

The golden age of the liturgy in the East and in the West [8]

Then came the golden age of the liturgy in the East and in the West, from 300 to about 900 A.D. The Fathers of the Church studied the celebration of the Eucharist from various aspects, especially as the presentation of the Passion, death, and Resurrection of Jesus. They explained how the faithful should participate in it, namely, by the offering of their own beings and by living their lives in charity.

This period saw the birth of the great liturgical communities around the patriarchal sees. The celebration no longer had the domestic and homelike appearance of a supper, but turned into a solemn ceremony which went together with a clearer understanding of the grandeur of the rite.

Deep theological maturity and spiritual riches were expressed in the "Eucharistic prayers" (or canons) which become fixed and obligatory. Even if they were said by the bishop or by a priest appointed by him, they were always an expression of the entire ecclesial community. This was the reason for the use of the plural "we."

The Eucharistic prayers, even in their variety, remained constant in some essential features: (a) thanksgiving and praise to the Father for having sent Christ to accomplish the salvation of humankind; (b) invocation of the Father, that he send the Holy Spirit to consecrate the bread and the wine and then to sanctify those participating; (c) commemoration of the Last Supper, which renews each time Christ's sacrifice, to which the entire Church unites its own sacrifice; and (d) remembrance of the saints in heaven, expressing the communion with the whole Church, and asking their intercession for the whole world.

The instructions following the Second Vatican Council have added to the Roman Canon three other Eucharistic prayers taken from the liturgy of this golden age. We will use as an example the second Eucharistic prayer, which developed from the anaphora of Hippolytus (230 A.D.) and is called "the Canon of the Age of the Martyrs."[9] We find in it part (a) devoted to thanksgiving and praise to the Father:

> Father, it is our duty and our salvation...
> to give you thanks
> through your beloved son Jesus Christ.
> He is...the Savior you sent to redeem us.
> [Through this mystery of salvation]
> we join the angels and saints
> in proclaiming your glory
> as we sing (say):
> Holy, holy, holy Lord....

(b) We come to the invocation of the Father that he send the Holy Spirit:

> Let your Spirit come upon these gifts to make
>   them holy,
> So that they may become for us
> the body and blood of our Lord, Jesus Christ.

And later this is added:

> May all of us who share in the body and blood of
>   Christ
> be brought together in unity by the Holy Spirit.

(c) There is the commemoration of the Last Supper:

> ...he took bread and gave you thanks.
> He broke the bread,
> gave it to his disciples, and said:
> Take this all of you and eat it:
> This is my body which will be given up for you.
> ...Do this in memory of me.

(d) Finally, we see expressed the communion of the whole Church on earth and in heaven:

Lord, remember your Church throughout the
   world;
make us grow in love,
together with ...our Pope...
Remember our brothers and sisters
who have gone to their rest
in the hope of rising again...
Have mercy on us all;
make us worthy to share eternal life
with Mary the Virgin Mother of God,
with the apostles,
and with all the saints...

The Eucharist in the West during the Middle Ages

The fundamental format of the Mass had been defined and
solidified. Now it was necessary to bring out another aspect
of the Eucharist: the real presence of Jesus and his personal
relationship with each of us. God's providence makes use of
everything to manifest the truth.

In the Eucharist Jesus is not understood any better than
when he was on earth.

The great schism of the Eastern Church and the political
developments of the time had an influence on the liturgy, for
it lost much of its popular and communitarian character. The
Eucharistic prayer was recited in such a way that the faithful
could hardly hear it. Communion was given under only one
species. Private Masses multiplied. The faithful began to
desert communion. The figure of the priest became too prominent. For some allegorists the celebration of the Mass became
nothing more than a representation of the Passion and death
of the Lord with strangely dramatic ceremonies and gestures.
The liturgical crisis was accompanied by the dogmatic one
which went so far as to deny the presence of Christ in the
Eucharist.

But then came the triumph of the Holy Spirit, who makes

all things work together for the good of the Church. The Church showed a reaction through its faith in the real presence of Christ in the Eucharist. This gave birth to the ritual worship of the Eucharist in itself. The feast of Corpus Christi was introduced with benedictions, expositions and processions of the Blessed Sacrament.

People found in the adoration of the Blessed Sacrament, the most meaningful way of celebrating the Eucharist. Thomas Aquinas became the theologian and the singer of the personal presence of Christ, true God and true man, in the Eucharist.

From the Council of Trent to the current liturgical renewal

The year 1500 brought in the era of the Protestant Reformation which repudiated the adoration of the Eucharist and the sacrifice of the Mass. At the same time, through the Council of Trent the Holy Spirit strongly affirmed the truth of the real presence and of the sacrifice of Christ in the Mass. On the real presence, the Council of Trent taught the following:

> "After the consecration of the bread and wine, our Lord Jesus Christ, true God and true Man, is really, truly, and substantially contained under those outward appearances." In this way, the Savior in his humanity is present not only at the right hand of the Father according to the natural manner of existence, but also in the sacrament of the Eucharist "by a mode of existence which we cannot express in words, but which, with a mind illumined by faith, we can conceive, and must most firmly believe, to be possible to God."[10]

Regarding the Mass as the sacrifice of Christ, the Council affirmed that "through the mystery of the Eucharist, the sacrifice of the cross, which was once offered on Calvary, is remarkably re-enacted and constantly recalled, and its saving power exerted for the forgiveness of those sins we daily commit."[11]

In the last four centuries the importance given to the adoration of the Blessed Sacrament and communion was an indication of the greater understanding of the Eucharistic mystery. Even communion was considered more as worship of Christ who is present, than as participation in the Eucharistic banquet. There followed different manifestations of this worship of Jesus in the Eucharist: Forty Hours devotions, visits to the Blessed Sacrament, Eucharistic Congresses. Congregations and religious institutes whose members were dedicated to the adoration of the Blessed Sacrament, were founded. Included among them are the Blessed Sacrament Fathers and the spiritual families of Charles de Foucauld.

This was a time in which the truths of the faith and the commitment to the Christian life were kept alive to such an extent as to create masterpieces of sanctity in many persons.

The Eucharist in our age

Then came our own age. Without losing an appreciation of what the people understand, the Church, which comprehends the whole and gives the right value to everything, used its teaching authority to bring back into balance aspects of the liturgy which had lost clarity and popularity. All this was done without ignoring what the majority of people had already understood.

The invitations of Pope Pius X to frequent communion and to communion for children were the prelude of a new era. The liturgical renewal, which developed first in Belgium and then in Germany, lead to a rediscovery of the theological and pastoral values of the Eucharist. This renewal drew from the sources of primitive liturgy, the writings of the Fathers of the Church, and from Scripture.

At the same time, the persecutions suffered by Christians in

Germany which compelled them to live a catacomb life, prompted them to relive with joy the primitive Eucharistic liturgies.

Pius XII in his encyclical *Mediator Dei* (1947) reconciled what was old and new in the Church and especially with regard to the Eucharistic liturgy. In the last few years with the Second Vatican Council and the encyclical *Mysterium Fidei* (1965) of Paul VI, all aspects of the celebration of the Mass have been brought back into the light: the Eucharist as a memorial, as the sacrifice of Jesus and of the Church, and as a banquet of communion with Christ and with our brothers and sisters. The Mass has acquired simpler and more home-like forms with a greater participation by the people. It has reflected the commitment to charity and to communion which fits in with modern needs particularly well.

The Second Vatican Council says:

> At the last Supper, on the night when he was betrayed, Our Savior instituted the Eucharistic Sacrifice of his Body and Blood. He did this in order to perpetuate the sacrifice of the Cross throughout the centuries until He should come again, and so to entrust to his beloved spouse, the Church, a memorial of his death and resurrection: a sacrament of love, a sign of unity, a bond of charity, a paschal banquet in which Christ is consumed, the mind is filled with grace, and a pledge of future glory is given to us.
>
> The Church therefore earnestly desires that Christ's faithful, when present at this mystery of faith, should not be there as strangers or silent spectators. On the contrary, through a proper appreciation of the rites and prayers, they should participate knowingly, devoutly, and actively. They should be instructed by God's word and be refreshed at the table of the Lord's body; they should give thanks to God by offering the Immaculate Victim, not only through the hands of the priest but also together with him, they should learn to offer themselves too. Through Christ the mediator, they should be drawn day by day into ever closer union with God and with each other, so that finally God may be all in all.[12]

Reading these passages on the liturgy of our times, I found the answer to a question I had often asked myself: What characterizes or is special about the Focolarini who have become priests after living for years a life of total sharing of possessions and of mutual love with the members of their community? And the answer was difficult because what they have is too simple. Now I am beginning to understand: they are the priests the Church wants today. Love has led them to break down every barrier between them and their brothers. Therefore they celebrate Mass either in the Focolare community where they live or on the occasion of large gatherings (conventions, Mariapolises*) of thousands of persons. The people attending are already united with them in the name of Jesus, as they ought to be.

In fact, the introduction to the new Sunday missal says,

> From the first moment of their meeting, Christians who come from different places and environments ought to recognize each other as brothers. Their unity is created by Christ present in their midst. He indeed has said: Where two or three are gathered in my name there am I in their midst (Mt 18:20).[13]

The rite of a Mass celebrated in a Focolare community is simple and homelike. The Mass involves everyone and not only the priest. Those who are readers prepare themselves well. Songs are carefully selected; for instance, the entrance song expresses the joy of the assembling community. People spontaneously express their intentions at the prayer of the faithful. And the priest is there at the center to renew in Christ's name the sacrifice of the cross.

The presence of Jesus among the participants touches the hearts of the people, who arrive at the most difficult decisions

*The Mariapolis is an annual meeting organized by the entire Focolare to build together a "temporary city"—the city of Mary.

as if they were alone with Jesus present on the altar. Once a child told me: "During Mass I felt as if I were with Jesus alone." This means that the community was one soul with the priest and with Christ on the altar and nothing disturbed that unity. Mass is the center and the high point of our meetings. Everything is a preparation for this personal encounter with Christ, and almost all the participants receive the Eucharist. After this, the assembly is filled with joy which bears witness to their unity with the risen Christ.

At the end of Mass, the priest and faithful leave as though in a continuation of the Mass itself. They go in order to bring charity into their homes, offices, factories—all their environments. There, the communion continues and sets people free. They go out to encourage other human beings to go ahead, whatever the circumstances and whatever their place in the whole world; this becomes an obligation in order to love as Jesus loved.

This is the people of God which is more of God now, where the sharing of goods is silent but constant and growing and serving a thousand needs; where communion with Christ grows in the living of his word, where longing for evangelization inflames people's hearts.

These are our priests: completely united with the people of God, representatives of the people at the altar, vicars of Christ who is the head of his body, Christ himself in his holy memorial. Our priests are...priests. Theirs is an extraordinary adventure.

UNITY WITH CHRIST
AND WITH OUR NEIGHBORS

In the previous chapters we have brought together and explained a little the Scripture passages concerning the institution of the Eucharist. We have considered also the liturgical and dogmatic development of the Eucharist throughout the centuries. After all this, we might get the impression that we have said everything. But what depths are hidden in the words of God! They contain God himself.

The Eucharist unites us to Christ

Let us see now the difference between the union with God which the Eucharist brings about and that which is the effect of other sacraments.

Other sacraments join us to Jesus through their own power, that is, through the specific grace that each sacrament gives. For example, the sacrament of matrimony gives the grace a person needs to live in unity with Christ in married life.

In the Eucharist, however, we are united to Jesus himself substantially present, because in the Eucharist we eat his flesh and drink his blood, as John says (cf. Jn 6:53-56).

Baptism, in which water is used to signify the washing away of original sin and other sins, is the sacrament of new birth. It is something personal, and it is received only once in a lifetime.

The Eucharist is food. And food is taken every day in order to maintain and to increase life. Thomas Aquinas says:

This sacrament is given under the form of food and drink. Therefore every effect which is produced for physical life by material food and drink, that is sustenance, growth, regeneration and pleasure, all of these effects are produced by this sacrament for the spiritual life.... [1] As physical food is necessary for life, so much so that one cannot live without it...so also spiritual food is necessary for the spiritual life, so much so that without it, one's spiritual life cannot be maintained. [2]

Thomas Aquinas also says that the one who does the generating (as Christ in baptism) makes the one generated (the human person) into his image, but does not assimilate him or her into his own substance. [3]

The Eucharist, however, produces a union of the faithful with God which goes far beyond that produced by baptism; it achieves a substantial assimilation. All of this, of course, has to be understood in such a way that we respect the distance between creator and creature. There is no physical fusion between the communicant and Christ; there is a mystical assimilation, spiritual but real, which allows one precisely to use the term *body,* one body. [4]

In the documents of Vatican II we read that communion with the body and blood of Christ does nothing less than change us into what we received. [5] This has been demonstrated by the great heights of mystical experience, by the transforming union that some saints have reached precisely through communion. Because the union between Christ and his Church is so complete, it has the character of a marriage; and this deep unity is also experienced in the union between Christ and the individual soul.

Having said this, we can understand the amazing statement of Thomas Aquinas: "The proper effect of the Eucharist is the transformation of the human person into God," one's divinization. [6]

When we read the works of the Fathers and the saints, we find that they reveal to us the reality of the Eucharist and its effects on persons receiving it with the proper disposition, in a very new way.

We expressed an intuition of this reality in a talk to the first international school for Focolarini* in 1961. Among other things, I said then:

> *God became a man in order to save us. When he had become a man, however, he desired to become food so that, feeding ourselves on him, each of us might become another Jesus. Now, it is one thing to see Jesus as if we had lived in his times; it is another thing to re-live Jesus, to be able to be another Jesus upon earth today. The Eucharist has precisely this purpose: to nourish us with Jesus in order to transform us into another Jesus because he has loved us as himself.*

We Christians have spoken and heard too many words with too little understanding of the love of Christ for us: "As the Father has loved me, so I have loved you" (Jn 15:9). That word "as" is really true. That is how we are loved. And so we can be other Christs, by means of the Eucharist. Do we realize it? If we realized it, by now the world would have been changed.

Jesus in the Eucharist, give me the grace, as I read the Fathers of your Church and your saints, to make you a little better known. This is the longing I feel in these days. I am almost distressed at my inadequacy, at my inability to express what you have given me to experience when close to you. It is too great. May the Holy Spirit make up for what I am unable to do, better yet, may he take over completely. He has a lot to do with the Eucharist.

Here is what we discovered in Cyril of Jerusalem: "In the figure of bread his body is given to you, and in the figure of

*Refer to footnote on page 84.

wine, his blood, that by partaking of the body and blood of Christ you may become one body and one blood with him."

We can speak of one body and blood not because a physical union is brought about, but because of the union of our persons with the glorified body of Christ, which is present in the Eucharist and is vivified by the Holy Spirit. We are, therefore, really one body, but in a new and mystical sense.

Cyril continues, "For when his body and blood become absorbed into the members of our bodies, we become Christ-bearers, so that, as St. Peter said, we become 'sharers of the divine nature' (2 P 1:4)."[7]

And Leo the Great: "For nothing else is brought about by the partaking of the body and blood of Christ than that we become what we eat; and both in spirit and in body we carry about everywhere Christ in whom and with whom we were dead, buried, and risen again."[8]

Augustine too writes as if he had heard a voice from on high: "I am the food of grown men: grow great and you shall eat of me. And you shall not change me into yourself as bodily food, but you shall be changed into me."[9]

And Doctor of the Church, Albert the Great, writes in several different works:

> This sacrament changes us into the body of Christ, in order that we may be bone of his bones, flesh of his flesh, and members of his members.[10]
>
> Every time two things are united in such a way that one has to be changed into all of the other, then the stronger transforms into itself that which is weaker. Therefore, since this food possesses greater power than those who eat of it, this food transforms into itself those who eat it.[11]
>
> Those who have received him [Jn 1:12] in the sacrament, eating him spiritually, become of one body with his Son, and so they are and they are called sons of God.
>
> In this generation the Lord's Body is like a seed which uses its power to attract man to itself and transform him into itself.
>
> How much we must thank Christ who with his life-giving

142

Body changes us into himself in order that we may become his holy body pure and divine.[12]

Next we will mention the writings of a few saints. Taking them by themselves they might perhaps seem exaggerated, sentimental, even insane. But the Fathers confirm their words and confirm that they are saints.

St. Thérèse of Lisieux tells how she met with Jesus: "That day it was no longer a *glance* but a *fusion*. There were no longer *two*. Therese had vanished like a drop of water in the ocean. Only Jesus remained. He was the master, he the king."[13] This experience ought not to be an isolated case reserved for exceptional souls. It ought to be and to become more of a common experience for all Christians if they receive communion with all the necessary conditions we will mention in the next chapter.

We have persons in the Focolare who are witnesses to this because they have lived intensely all that was required for the Eucharist to produce its full effect. God made them understand that they had become one with Christ. As a consequence of this, they were urged by the Holy Spirit to utter the word, "Abba—Father," as St. Paul said (cf. Gal 4:6).

As a matter of fact, A. Stolz says in his book on mystical theology:

> In the Eucharist there is achieved sacramentally the highest possible association with Christ in the sense of a complete transformation of our sinful being into the glorified being of Christ. Oneness with Christ frees us from our sinful being. In a sacramental mode...Christ lifts those who are assimilated and formed to himself out of the confines of time and conducts them before the face of the Father.... Participation in the Eucharist gives the believer his personal rapture. Out of this world at this stage, he is led by the Son to the Father in the region of the angels, and in union with the Son he is able to stand before the Father and address him as Father.[14]

St. Thérèse writes, " 'My heaven' is hidden in the particle where Jesus my spouse hides himself out of love.... What a divine moment it is when, my dearly beloved, in your tender affection you come to transform me into you. This union of love and of unutterable bliss, 'this is my heaven.' "[15]

Once more Thérèse speaks: "Jesus...transforms a white particle into himself every morning in order to communicate his life to you. What's more, with a love that is greater still, he wants to transform you into himself."[16]

And St. Peter Julian Eymard:

> This is an inexpressible union which comes next to the hypostatic union.... Why did Jesus Christ want to form such a union with us? To console us with his friendship, to enrich us with his graces, his merits. Above all, with the union of our lives with his and his with ours, he wanted to deify us in himself and thus fulfill the desire of the heavenly Father to crown him also in us, the members of his mystical body.[17]

The Eucharist and the resurrection of the body

Now we pass on to another effect which the Eucharist produces in the person who receives it under the proper conditions. We have already referred to it: the Eucharist is a cause of the resurrection of the flesh.

We are passing through times of great poverty of faith and times which are really bizarre in the substitutes they find for genuine faith. So we return to our Fathers, to great figures of all times, and to the pope, in order to see how they interpreted or interpret now those words of Jesus which in themselves are so clear.

Irenaeus says:

> Since the cup and bread become the word of God, and the Eucharist becomes the blood and the body of Christ, from which the very substance of our flesh is increased and

144

supported, how can they [the gnostics] claim that our flesh is incapable of receiving God's gift of eternal life, when our flesh is nourished from the body and the blood of the Lord and is a member of him?

Irenaeus continues:

> Just as a cutting from the vine planted in the ground bears fruit in its season, or as a grain of wheat falling into the earth and decomposing rises...so also our bodies which have been nourished by the Eucharist, when they are buried in the earth and decompose, shall arise at their appointed time, because the word of God raises them up to the glory of God the Father, who freely gives to this mortal body immortality, and to this corruptible body incorruption, because the strength of God is made perfect in weakness (cf. 1 Cor 15:53; 2 Cor 12:9).[18]

Justin, who agrees with Irenaeus of Lyons and Ignatius of Antioch on the idea that the Eucharist is a pledge of immortality and resurrection, expresses himself, according to some commentators, "as if the Eucharist already in this life rendered our bodies immortal and had actually initiated us into the resurrection."[19]

Origen too affirms, "it communicates its own immortality (for the Word of God is immortal) to the one who eats thereof."[20]

Thomas Aquinas writes:

> It is proper to attribute this effect to the sacrament of the Eucharist because, as Augustine says, the word resuscitates souls but the Word made flesh enlivens bodies. It is not just the Word and his Divinity that is present in this sacrament, but the Word united to his flesh as well, and therefore it is a cause of resurrection not only for souls but also of bodies.[21]

In his Easter message for 1976 Paul VI said, "Christ the Lord is truly risen.... We also brethren and sons and daughters, we also will rise!...if with a pure and

145

sincere heart we have fulfilled our Easter duty...for, of
the one that is fed with this vital food, Christ has said:
'I will raise him up on the last day' (Jn 6:54)."[22]

The Eucharist and the transformation of the cosmos

But the effect of the Eucharist in the human person
goes further than that. For, as St. Paul says: "The whole
created world eagerly awaits the revelation of the sons of
God...the world itself will be freed from its slavery to
corruption and share in the glorious freedom of the
children of God" (Rm 8:19,20). And this means that
creation too is called somehow to glory.

Jesus who dies and rises again is certainly the real
cause of the transformation of the cosmos. To
accomplish the renewal of the cosmos, however, Jesus
also expects the cooperation of people "Christified" by
his Eucharist. In fact, Paul tells us that through our
sufferings we complete "what is lacking in the sufferings
of Christ" (cf. Col 1:24) and that nature "awaits the revelation of the sons of God" (Rm 8:19). One could say,
therefore, that by means of the Eucharistic bread a
person becomes "eucharist" for the universe, in the sense
that joined with Christ he or she is the germ of the
transfiguration of the universe.

Actually, if the Eucharist is the cause of the resurrection of the human person, is it not possible that the
human body, divinized by the Eucharist, may be
destined to decay underground in order to contribute to
the renewal of the cosmos? We can say, therefore, that
after we have died with Jesus we are the Eucharist for
the earth. The earth eats us up as we eat the Eucharist,
indeed not in order to transform us into earth but to
transform the earth into "new heavens and a new earth"
(Rv 21:1).

It is a fascinating thought that the bodies of our Christian dead have the task of collaborating with God in the transformation of the cosmos. This generates in our hearts deep affection and veneration for those who have preceded us. It gives us a better understanding of the age-old custom of venerating those whom we call the dead (especially saints' bodies) since they are really coming to a new life in the cosmos.

The Eucharist redeems us and makes us God. We, after dying, cooperate with Christ in the transformation of nature, so that nature turns out to be like an extension of the body of Jesus. In fact Jesus, through the incarnation, took on human nature, which is where all of nature's elements meet.

The Eucharist and communion with our neighbors

Now let us contemplate the second chief effect of the Eucharist: that extraordinary divine fruitfulness we have talked about is produced not only in individuals; the Eucharist, as a true "sacrament of unity," also produces unity among people. And this is logical. If two persons are similar to a third, that is to Christ, they are similar to each other.

The Eucharist results in communion among brothers and sisters. And this is a glorious thing. If all of humankind took it seriously, this would have unimaginable consequences. For, if we understand that the Eucharist makes us one with each other, it becomes logical to treat all people as brothers and sisters. The Eucharist forms the family of the children of God, all brothers and sisters of Jesus and of each other.

The natural family has its laws. If these were extended to a supernatural level and applied on a vast scale, they would change the world. In the family everything is shared: life itself, the house, the furniture.... A good family has its own intimacy; its members know one another's joys and sorrows because they communicate them. When they go out into the world they convey the warmth of their own home. They can benefit the rest of society if they reflect the integrity of a wholesome family. A family is happy when its members come together for a meal or when they sing or play together.

If the family is one of the creator's most beautiful works, what must the family of God's children be like?

In the Middle East, the common meal was given great importance. Not only did Jesus want to have his closest disciples around him at the Last Supper; but when he shared his own cup with them and broke his own bread for them, he seemed to be wanting to draw them closer to himself, almost to unite them with his own person. Jesus shows us with these external signs that the Eucharist is the sacrament of unity.

Another stupendous thing about the banquet of Jesus is that he elevated it to the level of an infinitely superior reality.

By means of the Eucharist he united Christians to himself and to each other into one single body, which is his own body. As a result, he gave the Church its most intimate and essential life: the Church is the body of Christ, and reflects brotherhood, unity, life, and communion with God.

The Eucharist, therefore, brings about the Church, and not just part of it but the entire Church. It is the complete body of Christ present in a given place, as the letter of Paul makes clear: "to the Church of God which is in Corinth" (1 Cor 1:2).

The Eucharist also makes all of the members of the mystical body present, even though distances of space and separation by death may seem to divide them. Distance in space and time are nonexistent in the glorious Christ present there.

It is stated in the documents of Vatican II, "Celebrating the

Eucharistic sacrifice, therefore, we are most closely united to the worshipping Church in heaven."[23]

In the Acts of the Apostles, we see how the Eucharist immediately helped Christians to become aware of being a single body: "The community of believers were of one heart and one mind. None of them ever claimed anything of his own; rather, everything was held in common" (Ac 4:32).

And John of Damascus writes that the Eucharist "is called *communion,* and truly is so, because of our having communion through it with Christ... and because through it we have communion with and are united to one another.... We all become one body of Christ and one blood and members of one another."[24]

Origen too says that whoever partakes of the Eucharist must become aware of what "communion with the Church" means. One of his commentators observes: "Communion with the body of Christ is communion with his bread but at the same time with his Church. The reality of the Eucharistic assembly and of each of its participants is not less important than the reality of the Eucharistic bread."[25]

Albert the Great emphasizes this reality in several passages:

> As the bread, the matter of this sacrament, is made into one loaf out of many grains which share their entire makeup, penetrating each other, so the true body of Christ is put together from many drops of blood of our own nature...mixed together; and thus many believers...united in sentiment and communicating mystically with Christ their head, constitute the body of Christ.... That is why this sacrament leads us to effect a communion of all our goods temporal and spiritual.[26]
>
> The species of this sacrament, in other words, bread and wine, are symbols of communion, which means the union of many in one, because bread is prepared out of many grains and wine from many grapes.[27]
>
> By the very fact that Christ unites all to himself, he unites them with each other, because if several things are united to a third they are united also with one another.[28]

149

In conclusion, Albert the Great affirms, that the true body of Christ is the cause of the unity of the mystical body. The special effect of the Eucharist is the grace of incorporation, which is the supreme degree of union.[29]

The Holy Father Paul VI has some incomparable expressions on the Eucharist. I will quote just one:

> The Eucharist...has been instituted to make us brothers...so that from being strangers scattered far and wide and indifferent to one another, we become united, equal, and friends. It is given to change us from an apathetic and egoistic mass, from being people divided and hostile to each other, into a people, a real people, believing and loving, of one heart and of one soul.[30]

The Eucharist and the ideal of unity

Ours is the ideal of unity. Now, is it not significant that Jesus, in his famous prayer to the Father, should ask for unity among his disciples and among those to come, right after having instituted the Eucharist which made that unity possible?

This is how Jesus prayed while walking towards the Garden of Olives (Jn 17:11-23).

> O Father most holy,
> protect them with your name which you have
> given me,
> that they may be one, even as we are one.

The unity between the Father and the Son is the model for our own. And we can be one as they are one because of the Eucharist.

> I do not pray for them alone.
> I pray also for those who will believe in me
> through their word,

150

> that all may be one
> as you, Father, are in me and I in you;
> I pray that they may be one in us,
> that the world may believe that you sent me.

Through the Eucharist we are in Jesus, who is in the Father.

> I have given them the glory you gave me
> that they may be one, as we are one—
> I living in them, you living in me—
> that their unity may be complete.

We do not enter into the kingdom unless the unity we achieve with Jesus and with one another through the Eucharist is similar to the unity between the Father and the Son.

If we love our great ideal, our vocation to unity, we must have an immense love for the Eucharist.

THE EUCHARIST AND HUMANITY

Conditions for the Eucharist to produce its full effect.

We have considered the tremendous effects produced by the Eucharist. It is logical that they should come about in a believer if certain conditions are fulfilled.[1]

Our incorporation into Christ, our personal deification, our complete unity with the Church, all depend on our disposition when we receive communion.

When we read the Didache and the early Fathers of the Church in general, we discover that the basic conditions are the following: to believe in the doctrine of Christ; to be baptized; in particular, to have faith in what the Eucharist is; to live in accordance with the teachings of Christ; to repent and to confess one's own sins in order to approach the Eucharist with a pure heart; to be reconciled with those brethren one might not be at peace with; to be in unity with the Church, with the bishop; to desire that union with Christ and with one's neighbors that the Eucharist brings about.

It is written in the Didache:

> Let no one eat or drink of the Eucharist with you except those baptized in the name of the Lord, for it was in reference to this that the Lord said: "Do not give that which is holy to dogs" (Mt 7:6)...On the Lord's Day, after you have come together, break bread and offer the Eucharist, having first confessed your offenses, so that your sacrifice may be pure. But let no one who has a quarrel with his neighbor join you until he is reconciled, lest your sacrifice be defiled.[1]

We call this food the Eucharist, declares Justin, of which only he can partake who has acknowledged the truth of our teachings, who has been cleansed by Baptism for the remission of his sins and for his regeneration, and who regulated his life upon the principles laid down by Christ.[2]

John Chrysostom says:

> In the [Eucharistic] mysteries let us not limit our attention to what falls in the range of our senses, but let us keep in mind his words.... The Word said, "This is my body" (Mt 26:26). And so we must submit ourselves and believe; we must look at this with the eyes of faith. Christ has given us nothing tangible.... All his gifts are spiritual realities, though contained in things that are tangible.... For if you were incorporeal, he would have given you these incorporeal gifts without any perceptible signs; but in fact your soul is joined to your body; and so he gives you these spiritual realities in things that are tangible.[3]

Origen, commenting on this passage from Paul: "A man should examine himself first; only then should he eat of the bread" (1 Cor 11:28), says that "if anyone...does not obey these words, but in haphazard fashion participates in the bread of the Lord and his cup, he becomes weak or sickly or, even—if I may use the expression—stunned by the power of the bread, he drops dead."[4]

And Cyprian:

> God does not accept the sacrifice offered by one who nurses a grudge. He wants him to leave the altar and go first to be reconciled with his brother; for no one can make peace with God if he prays with hatred in his heart. The noblest sacrifice in the eyes of God is our peace, that is, harmony among brothers and a people gathered in the unity of the Father and of the Son and of the Holy Spirit.[5]

John Chrysostom says again:

> Therefore let no one be a Judas. . . . If you have anything against your enemy. . . put a stop to the hostility in order that you may be able to receive the medicine (that is, pardon) from this table. For you are approaching an awesome and holy sacrifice. Respect the meaning of this oblation. Christ lies there as the victim, and for whom and for what reason was he immolated? To join the things which belong there above to those that belong here below. . . to reconcile you with the God of the universe, to turn you from an enemy and an antagonist into a friend. . . . He did not refuse to die for you and do you refuse to pardon your own companion?. . . [This sacrifice] turns all of us into one single body since we all receive one body. Let us join therefore into one single body. . . uniting ourselves to one another with the bond of charity.[6]

Finally, Ignatius of Antioch: "A man who acts without the knowledge of the bishop is serving the devil."[7]

Next, we see that the great medieval theologians hand on the thought of the Fathers.

St. Albert the Great puts it like this: "Because of this charity which unites God with man and man with God, this sacrament is called the sacrament of unity and of charity. Therefore we must eat this supper in the charity of ecclesiastical unity."[8]

Thomas Aquinas says:

> In a false person the sacrament does not produce any effect. We are false when the inmost self does not correspond to what is expressed externally. The sacrament of the Eucharist is an external sign that Christ is incorporated into the one who receives him and he into Christ. One is false if in his heart he does not desire this union and does not even try to remove every obstacle to it; Christ therefore does not remain in him, neither does he in Christ.[9]

Making a kind of summary of the necessary spiritual dispositions, Paul VI says: "In the realm of the Eucharist he understands who believes and loves. Love becomes a co-efficient of intelligence because its object is finally possessed. For the conquest of divine things love is more effective than every other spiritual faculty we have."[10]

And so, whoever approaches the Eucharist and wants to be in tune with this sacrament, must be firmly decided to achieve in one's life that which the Eucharist signifies and achieves, namely unity.

Other effects of the Eucharist

Having considered what conditions are needed for receiving the extraordinary graces of the Eucharist, let us now give some thought to what the Eucharist brings our souls, besides the principal effect of making us one body with Christ and our brothers and sisters.

I have mentioned the fact that the Eucharist is also regarded by the Church as "food for the journey," food for the people of God who are on a pilgrimage towards their final end, and thus it is called *viaticum*. As such it endows our souls with an increase of love, with a consequent lessening of the passions, as Thomas Aquinas says.[11] It brings comfort in suffering and strength in battles and trials, until we arrive at sanctity and at eternal life.

It is the Eucharist which gives us "divine charity," "the light of wisdom," and "joy to our hearts and souls." "It stirs a person so much that it makes one go out of oneself and reach the point of no longer seeing self for self, but self for God, and God for God." These are the expressions of Catherine of Siena.[12]

And for St. Paul of the Cross the Eucharist is "that food of the angels which redounds also to the strengthening of the body."[13]

The Eucharist in the life of the Christian

Of course, Eucharistic communion is not an end in itself. "The union with Christ to which this sacrament is directed...has to be prolonged throughout the entire life of a Christian...."[14]

There is one reality of the Church that meets for the celebration of the Eucharist and manifests the *Ekklesia*. But there is another reality of the Church that is spread all over the world as a manifestation of Christ among people, as a sign of his presence.

The world does not receive the proclamation of Christ from the Eucharist so much as through the life of Christians nourished on the Eucharist and on the Word. Preaching the Gospel with their lives and with their voices, they render Christ present in the midst of human persons.[15]

If it is united to Jesus in the Eucharist, the Christian community can and must do what Jesus has done: give its life for the world.

The life of the Church, thanks to the Eucharist, becomes the life of Jesus, a life capable of giving love, the life of God, to others, and capable of saving, since it is the very life of Jesus that is carried over to the community and to every single member in it. In this sense, we can understand the words of Paul: "And you put me back in labor pains until Christ is formed in you" (Gal 4:19).

Paul VI says that the Lord "sought to join his divine life to ours in such an intimate and loving way as to give himself to us as our nourishment and thus make us share in a personal way in his redemptive sacrifice...[in order] that each one of us should be inserted into and carried along in his design of salvation—which is open to all of humankind."[16]

The great theologian, Emile Mersch, explains:

> The act by which Christ likens us to himself in the Eucharist is his sacrifice. The Eucharist has the tendency to make the

157

lives of Christians a sacrifice, so that the Cross may take possession of humankind. Christ offered full reparation for sin. The faithful also offer reparation, both for themselves as individuals and on behalf of the whole mystical body; theirs is a reparation proper to members, for it continues Christ's reparation, on which it depends and from which it derives.

Christ, the Redeemer, [Mersch continues] who assimilates Christians to Himself, is Christ in the greatest act of his love. His love impels him to perfect obedience to the Father and to the offering of himself as a holocaust for men [in his abandonment, we would say]. This love permeates Christians and transforms them into itself. . . . We honor [the Eucharist] more by devotedness to our fellow human beings than by ornate ceremonies, although the latter are also necessary.[17]

Furthermore, since modern theology has placed less emphasis on the presence of Jesus in the Eucharist, which the faithful are aware of already, than on spiritual union with him and with every member of his mystical body, Eucharistic spirituality too is directed today not so much towards the adoration of the present Lord as toward communion with him and with our brothers and sisters in every moment of the day.

The experience of the Focolare

But let's pause a moment. As we were reading these passages regarding the disposition we need for approaching the Eucharist and the effects that it produces, didn't you hear the Holy Spirit whispering in your hearts or, even more, didn't you feel like shouting out: "But this is our ideal! This is our ideal!" I confess that when I read all this I was astonished.

Do you remember, ever since we were first starting out, how carefully we prepared ourselves every morning for communion, making sure that the unity among us was perfect, and how we were ready to do without our communion if we did not pass the test of unity?

Do you remember how every morning we felt as if the Holy Spirit were knocking on the door of our spirits tirelessly repeating, "If you recall that your brother has anything against you, leave your gift at the altar, go first to be reconciled with your brother" (Mt 5:23-24)?

Do you remember our regular confessions and general confessions in order to give a better start to our new life?

And the faith we had in the Church that would permit no doubts?

And how like a banner headline above every other was the phrase, "He who hears you, hears me" (Lk 10:16), for in our bishop we saw Christ whom we must obey?

Remember how deeply rooted in us was the conviction that no penance, no sacrifice was greater than that of loving one another as Jesus has loved us, as Cyprian says?[18]

And there is really no need to add what Paul VI has affirmed, that love was our strength during our entire lives.[19]

As for the effects, do you remember how from the first, as our love was growing, the temptations that had tormented people for their entire lives, disappeared suddenly as if by magic; then after months or years the same temptations would reappear as trials from the Lord or as a result of a slackening of their love?

And how much comfort Jesus in the Eucharist brought us during our trials when no one would give us an audience because the Focolare was being evaluated by the Church. He was always there, at every hour of the day, waiting for us, telling us: after all, in the end, I am the one who is the head of the Church.

Both in our battles and in every sort of suffering, who gave us strength? We thought that we would have died many times if Jesus in the Eucharist and Jesus in our midst, nourished by the Eucharist, had not sustained us.

And the wisdom of which the Focolare has so much. And the smile that characterizes its members. And the heart so often on fire. And our living for God at all times, and our knowing and telling each other that we were the luckiest people in the world. Where does all this come from? Jesus in the Eucharist!

It was he who made our whole life a continuous "spiritual exercise"; — twenty-four hours a day we would never feel "down," and would always be quick to begin again if we had stopped.

Do you remember how, from the very beginning, after we met together for Mass, we would go out into all kinds of places — farms, schools, offices, and so on — to carry the news of Christ, of his new commandment, and of his Gospel? We did not just repeat the doctrine but told the experience of our new life.

And our program was not a limited one. It has always been focused on the phrase "that all may be one" (Jn 17:21). Our aim was the human race, knowing that to gain its salvation, we, like Jesus, had to pay with our lives first, and talk afterwards.

That we had to offer our lives was obvious. And whenever we were asked, we offered them for the same motive: for the Church, "that all may be one."

This life has been going on for more than thirty years in the Focolare; and during these days of meditating on the Eucharist, I often asked myself: but has the Eucharist always been the "motor" behind our whole life?

There is certainly a wonderful interconnection between the Eucharist and the ideal of unity. The fact that the Lord, to get this vast movement started, made us concentrate on the prayer of Jesus, on his last testament, means that he had to give us a strong push towards the only one who could accomplish it: Jesus in the Eucharist.

From the very beginning of the Focolare, we noted this phenomenon just as newborn babes instinctively feed at their mothers' breasts without knowing what they are doing, so those who got to know us began to go to communion every day.

How can we explain it? What instinct is for the newborn baby, the Holy Spirit is for an adult who has been born anew into the new life that the Gospel of unity brings. He or she is carried into the heart of Mother Church, nourished on the most precious nectar she has. Just look at the consequences.

Yes, this is our ideal, what in essence we have always been living, because our ideal is nothing but Christianity lived from the viewpoint of unity, the ideal of Christ.

The Eucharist and human society

And now I would not want to leave out another magnificent effect of the Eucharist, which Paul VI has sketched for us:

> This communion of supernatural life can have an enormous and immensely beneficial impact on every aspect of life in society. You know how this basic problem of humankind's social dimension towers above and dominates all others...how to build the earthly city. All of us know how people get caught up in this work of construction, and quite often, in fact, they manage to make remarkable progress.... And yet at every step they encounter obstacles and resistance within themselves simply because they lack any single transcendent principle to unify the human fabric.
>
> The earthly city has no reserves of faith and of love and it cannot find them in itself and of itself. But the religious city, the Church, existing within the earthly city, can supply those reserves through the tacit osmosis of example and spiritual virtue.[20]
>
> Isn't this perhaps the reason why the Eucharist is a sign to which our modern world should look with absolute trust? For it is constantly seeking and producing unity, then shattering and fragmenting it again, but always, almost in spite of itself, craving and reestablishing it; for unity, we declare, is the summit of its aspiration.[21]

The Eucharist and the Holy Spirit

And now, at the conclusion of these brief reflections on the Eucharist, I want to say a few more words about the Holy Spirit.

In his magnificent passage on the bread of life, John quotes Jesus as saying: "It is the spirit that gives life; the flesh is useless" (Jn 6:63). In this phrase Jesus refers to the role of the Holy Spirit in the Eucharistic mystery. The Holy Spirit is the principal agent every time Christ comes among us.[22] Through him the Word became flesh in Mary's womb, and it is through him that the Word becomes flesh in the host and becomes blood in the wine at the consecration of the Eucharist in every Mass.

Cyril of Jerusalem writes: "Next, after sanctifying ourselves by these spiritual songs, we ask God in his mercy to send his Holy Spirit upon our offering to make our bread the Body of Christ and our wine the Blood of Christ. For whatever the Holy Spirit touches is totally sanctified and transformed."[23]

Thus, the Mass proves to be a perpetuation of the incarnation. Surely, that is something worthy of our amazement and of our worship. The theologian, Betz, writes that the second-century thinkers adopt the mind of John, who "sees in the Eucharistic incarnation a sacramental continuation of Jesus' mission in the flesh."[24]

The flesh, therefore, on which we are nourished is a glorified flesh, the same flesh that Jesus possesses where he sits at the right hand of the Father. From this glorified flesh, which gives divine life, there is an outflowing of the Holy Spirit, who forms Christ in us because we have been fed with the Eucharist.

It is the Holy Spirit, therefore, who sanctifies us for eternal life. It is through the Holy Spirit that Jesus rises in glory after his death. It is he who comes down to build the Church, the body of Christ. Again, it is the Holy Spirit who brings about unity in the community and sanctifies the community. The

Holy Spirit is God, frequently silent yet continually at work, as powerfully active as he is little known; he is the Love that highlights the Father and the Son.

As I have already indicated, God's plan for the total Christ is a magnificent journey from the Trinity back to the Trinity.

The Father loves us and sends the Son; and among the things which the Son must accomplish in conjunction with the Father, is the Eucharist. If the Son is a gift from the Father to humankind, the Eucharist is a gift from that first gift. Now, when a person well disposed receives the Eucharist, being made one body with the son and with one's brothers and sisters, that person re-enters the bosom of the Father.

Here is what Vatican II says: "In this celebration the faithful, united with their bishop and endowed with an outpouring of the Holy Spirit, gain access to God the Father through the Son...they enter into communion with the most Holy Trinity."[25]

We know that there have been saints and other persons whom God has given a special task in the Church and to whom God reveals, in a more or less profound way, their immanence in the bosom of the Father.

Now generally it is not like this, not for everyone. Instead, it is being in the bosom of the Father and, at the same time, feeling a continuous longing to arrive there.

The Eucharist is food which refreshes, reinforces, and strengthens more and more, and we have to eat of it often to be able to say, "the life I live now is not my own; Christ is living in me" (Gal 2:20).

Jesus, when I set out to say something about you in the Eucharist, I think that my heart was almost on fire in my breast. I suddenly realized what I was about to do: to say something about you in four meager conversations. If I could have accomplished what I really desired, I would have built you a cathedral.

163

Now I feel the end result is nothing more, perhaps, than a little wooden altar. I am not capable of speaking of you. You are too great.

(I read once that if the Church did not have the Eucharist, it would not have the strength to rise up towards God, so that the Eucharist is considered to be the heart of the Church.)

And so, forgive my daring. But since your trick is to draw great things out of weakness, I offer you these pages as a tiny gift of love for your infinite gift of love. Use them so that others may know you a little better and understand how, with the strength they receive from you, they can unleash a Christian revolution in the world.

NOTES

PART I: OUR YES TO GOD

Chapter 1

1. Claus Westermann, *Genesis,* 1. Teilband: "Genesis 1-11," in *Biblischer Kommentar, Altes Testament* (Neukirchen, 1974), Vol. 1, 218.

Chapter 2

1. See the section devoted to this same topic in Chapter 3.
2. See Ephesians 4:22-24
3. Francis de Sales, *Treatise on the Love of God,* VIII, 7, trans. Henry Mackey, O.S.B. (Westminster: The Newman Bookshop, 1945), 340-341.
4. Catherine of Siena, Letter 5, in *Epistolario* (Alba, 1966), Vol. 2, 220.

Chapter 3

1. Maria Winowska, *The Death Camp Proved Him Real,* trans. Therese Plumereau (Kenosha: Prow Books, 1971), 31.
2. *Treatise on the Love of God,* VIII, 7, 340.
3. J.M. Perrin, O.P., *Catherine of Siena,* trans. Paul Barrett, O.F.M. Cap. (Westminster: Newman Press, 1965), 142.
4. Perrin, *Catherine of Siena,* 143.
5. Letter 132, in *Epistolario,* II, 489.
6. Teresa of Avila, *The Interior Castle,* II, 8, in *The Complete Works of St. Teresa of Avila,* trans. and ed. E. Allison Peers (New York: Sheed & Ward, 1950), Vol. 2, 301.
7. *The Foundations,* V, 10, in *The Complete Works,* Vol. 3, 23.

8. *Spiritual Relations,* XIX, in *The Complete Works,* Vol. 1, 344.

9. Paul of the Cross, Letter 162, *Letters of St. Paul of the Cross,* trans. by Passionist Fathers (Manuscript in Immaculate Conception Monastery Library, Jamaica, N.Y.), 162

10. Paul VI to the general audience, June 14, 1972, *The Teachings of Pope Paul VI: 1972* (Washington, D.C.: USCC, 1973), 83-84.

11. John XXIII, *Journal of a Soul,* trans. Dorothy White (New York: McGraw-Hill, 1965), 112.

12. Paul VI, Address on the feast of St. Joseph (March 19, 1968), *Insegnamenti di Paolo VI,* VI (Rome: Poliglotta Vaticana, 1969), 1154-1155.

13. Josemaría Escrivá de Balaguer, *The Way* (New York: Scepter, 1979), 176

14. *The Way,* 179.

15. *Lettere di San Paolo della Croce,* ed. Padre Amedeo della Madre del Buon Pastore (Rome, 1924), Vol.1, 491

16. John of the Cross, *The Ascent of Mount Carmel,* 21, 4, in *The Collected Works of St. John of the Cross,* trans. K. Kavanaugh and O. Rodriguez (Washington, D.C.: ICS Publications, 1973), Vol. 2, 174

17. St. Elizabeth of the Trinity, Letter 169, *J'ai trouvé Dieu,* Ib (Paris: Ed. du Cerf, 1980), 168.

18. General audience, March 12, 1969, *Teachings: 1969* (1970), 50.

19. General audience, August 25, 1971, *Teachings: 1971* (1972), 131.

20. Augustine, *Enarr. in Ps. (On the Psalms),* XXXII, 2, s.1, 2.

21. L. DiPinto, *Volontà del Padre,* in N.D.S. (Rome: Ed. Paoline, 1979), 1715.

22. *The Ascent of Mount Carmel,* II, 22, 3, in *The Collected Works,* 179.

23. Cyprian, *De dominica oratione (Treatise on the Lord's Prayer),* XV.

24. *St. Thérèse of Lisieux, Her last Conversations,* trans. John Clarke, O.C.D. (Washington, D.C.: ICS, 1977), 63.

25. St. Thérèse of Lisieux, *Story of a Soul,* trans. John Clarke, O.C.D. (Washington, D.C.: ICS, 1975), 27.

26. *Last Conversations,* 97-98.

27. St. Thérèse of Lisieux, *J'entre dans la vie* (Paris: Cerf-DDB, 1973), 235.

28. *Thoughts of Soeur Thérèse of the Child Jesus* (New York,

1915), 117.

29. *Declaration on Religious Freedom,* 14, in *The Documents of Vatican II,* ed. W.M. Abbott and J. Gallagher (New York: America Press, 1966), 694. Unless otherwise noted, all council quotes are taken from the edition here cited, and are used with permission of America Press, Inc., 106 W. 56th St., New York, N.Y. 10019 © 1966 All Rights Reserved.

30. *Dogmatic Constitution on the Church,* 13, in *The Documents,* 30.

31. *Pastoral Constitution on the Church in the Modern World,* 93, in *The Documents,* 307.

32. John Paul II to the American Bishops, October 5, 1979, U.S.A. — *The Message of Justice, Peace and Love* (Boston: St. Paul Editions, 1979), 187.

33. *The Church,* 41, in *The Documents,* 70.

34. *The Church in the Modern World,* 11, in *The Documents,* 209.

35. *The Church,* 21, in *The Documents,* 41-42.

36. See *Insegnamenti di Paolo VI,* II (Rome: Poliglotta Vaticana, 1965), 980.

37. *Decree on the Renewal of the Religious Life,* 14, in *Vatican II, The Conciliar and Post Conciliar Documents,* ed. Austin Flannery, O.P. (Wilmington, 1975), 619.

38. Veronica Giuliani, *Il mio calvario,* ed. P. Pizzicaria (Città di Castello, 1960), 126.

39. *The Church in the Modern World,* 16, in *The Documents,* 213.

40. General audience, August 9, 1972, *Insegnamenti di Paolo VI,* X (1973), 797-798.

41. Letter 151, *Epistolario,* II, 97.

42. St. Athanasius, *The Life of St. Anthony,* in *The Fathers of the Church, A New Translation,* ed. R. Deferrari (New York, 1952), Vol. 15.

43. *The Collected Letters of Thérèse of Lisieux,* ed. Abbé Combes, trans. F.J. Sheed (New York: Sheed & Ward, 1949), 102.

44. Thérèse of Lixieux, *Gli Scritti* (Rome, 1979), 818.

45. *J'entre dans la vie,* 48.

46. *Last Conversations,* 155.

47. *Last Conversations,* 241.

48. *The Letters of St. Frances Xavier Cabrini,* trans. Sr. Ursula

167

Infante, M.S.C. (New York, 1969), 8.
49. *Journal of a Soul,* 98

Chapter 4

1. St. Francis de Sales, *Treatise on the Love of God,* IX, 4, II (Garden City, 1963), 105.
2. Teresa of Avila, "Poesias," II, *Obras Completas,* 3rd Ed. (Madrid: Editorial Plenitud, 1964), 935-937.
3. Augustine, Letter 130, *Letters,* Vol. 2, in *The Fathers of the Church, A New Translation,* ed. R. Deferrari (New York, 1953), 397.
4. Augustine, *Tractatus in Johannis Evangelium (Homilies on the Gospel of John),* 25, 3.
5. Augustine, *Enarr. in Ps. (On the Psalms),* XXXVI, 2, 13.
6. *Enarr. in Ps.,* XXXV, 16.
7. See Prov. 3:11-12; Job 5:17; Rev. 3:19.
8. *The Interior Castle,* XXXII, 6-7, in *The Complete Works,* Vol. 2, 136-137.
9. *Lettere,* Vol. 1, 616-617.
10. John Bosco, *Scritti Spirituali,* ed. J. Aubry (Rome, 1976), Vol. 1, 151.
11. "Retreat: How to find heaven on earth," in *Sr. Elizabeth of the Trinity, Spiritual Writings,* trans. M.M. Philipon, O.P. (London: Geoffrey Chapman, 1962), 143.
12. "Letter to Louise Desmoulin," in *Spiritual Writings,* 107.
13. *The Way,* 168.
14. "Letter to Sano di Marco and others" (62), in Perrin, *Catherine of Siena,* 146.
15. Letter 75, in *Il messaggio di Santa Caterina da Siena, dottore della Chiesa,* ed. un missionario vincenziano (Rome, 1970), 717.
16. *The Way,* 177.
17. *The Way,* 178.
18. *The Foundations,* V, 7-8, in The Complete Works, Vol. 3, 21-22.
19. Conference 90, in *The Conferences of St. Vincent de Paul to the Daughters of Charity,* trans. Joseph Leonard, C.M. (Westminster: Newman Press, 1952), Vol. 4, 54.
20. Conference 24, in Conferences of St. Vincent de Paul, ed. Pierre Coste, C.M., trans. Joseph Leonard, C.M. (Philadelphia, 1963), 52.
21. Conference 199, in Coste, *Conferences,* 490.

22. Conference 48, in *Conferences to the Daughters of Charity,* 175.
23. *Lettere,* Vol. 2, 264
24. *Lettere di san Paolo della Croce,* ed. C. Chiari (Rome, 1977), Vol. 5, 191.
25. Letter 260, in *Lettere di santa Francesca Saverio Cabrini* (Milan, 1968), 563.
26. Letter 643, in *Sainte Louis de Marillac, Ses Ecrits* (Paris, 1961), 775.
27. *The Way of Perfection,* XXXII, 12, in *The Complete Works,* Vol. 2, 138-139.
28. *Tractatus in Johannis Evangelium (Homilies on the Gospel of John),* 10, 3.
29. G. Domanski, "IL pensiero mariano di Massimiliano Kolbe," *Quaderni della Milizia dell'Immacolata,* Vol. 4 (1971), 79.
30. Letter 340, in *Il messaggio,* 714.
31. *Lettere di san Paolo della Croce,* ed. Amedeo, Vol. 1, 49.
32. *Lettere,* ed. p. Amedeo, Vol. 1, 611.
33. *U.S.A. — The Message of Justice, Peace and Love,* 137.
34. *Spiritual Writings,* 102.
35. Conference 199, in Costc, *Conferences,* 497-498.
36. *Ses Ecrits,* 895.
37. *Ses Ecrits,* 896.
38. Letter 144, in *Ses Ecrits,* 190.
39. Maximilian Kolbe, "Scritti," in *Solo l'amore crea,* ed. G. Barra (Turin, 1972), 49.
40. *Il mio calvario,* 196.
41. Francis de Sales, *Tutte le lettere* (Rome, 1967), Vol. 1, 662.
42. *Tutte le lettere,* 789.
43. *Scritti Spirituali,* Vol. 2, 111.
44. The Curé of Ars, *Scritti scelti,* ed. Gérard Rossé (Rome: Città Nuova, 1975), 76.
45. *Last Conversations,* 290.
46. *Journal of a Soul,* 84.
47. *Decree on the Ministry and Life of Priests,* 14, in *The Documents,* 562.
48. *Insegnamenti di Paolo VI,* VI (1969), 1155.
49. Paul VI, "Pensiero alla morte," *Osservatore Romano,* 5 August 1979, 5.
50. *Spiritual Writings,* 102.
51. Clement of Rome, "First Letter," 20, in *Early Christian Fathers,* ed. and trans. Cyril C. Richardson (New York:

Macmillan, 1970), 53.

52. Peter Chrysologus, *Sermones (Sermons)*, 72.

Chapter 5

1. Alphonsus de Liguori, *Uniformity with God's Will,* trans. Thomas W. Tobin, C.SS.R., copyright ©1952. Reprinted with permission of the Redemptorist Fathers, Brooklyn, N.Y. The following references all refer to this work unless otherwise indicated.
2. 4.
3. Vincent de Paul, Letter 3008, in *Correspondance, Entretiens, Documents,* ed. Pierre Coste, C.M. (Paris, 1923), Vol. 8, 151.
4. 5-6.
5. Alphonsus Liguori, *Pratica di amare Gesù Cristo* (Rome, 1973), 173-174.
6. 6.
7. 6.
8. 7.
9. 7.
10. 8-9.
11. 9-10.
12. 14-15.
13. 11.
14. *Pratica di amare Gesù Cristo,* 175-180.
15. 12.
16. 16.
17. *Pratica di amare Gesù Cristo,* 181.
18. 17-19.
19. 23-24.
20. 26-27.
21. 28-29.
22. Alphonsus Liguori, *Affetti divoti a Gesù Cristo,* in *Opere ascetiche* (Rome, 1933), Vol. 1, 384-385.

PART II: THE WORD OF LIFE

Chapter 1

1. St. Augustine, "In Johannis Evangelium, Tractatus CVI," in *Corpus Christianorum, Series Latina, XXXVI* (Turnholdt, 1955), 53.
2. Cf. Justin Martyr, *The Dialogue with Trypho,* trans. A. Lukyn Williams, (New York: Macmillan, 1930), Ch. 8, 6:491d.
3. St. Gregory of Nazianzus, *Poemata ad Alios: VII (Ad Nemesium),* Vols. 37-49, 37:1533a.
4. St. Basil, Bishop of Caesarea, "Epistle 223," in *Correspond ence* (Torino: Societa Editrice Internazionale, 1983).
5. St. Justin Martyr, *Second Apology,* Ch. 10; 6:459b.
6. St. Justin Martyr, *Trypho,* ibid.
7. St. Thèrése of Lisieux, *Autobiography,* trans. Ronald Knox (New York: Kennedy, 1958), 218.
8. St. Teresa of Avila, *The Way of Perfection,* trans. E. Allison Peers (New York: Doubleday, 1964), 151.
9. St. Bonaventure, *Collations on the Six Days,* (Collation 19), 7.
10. St. Gertrude the Great, *Exercises* (Westminster, Md: Newman Press, 1956), V.
11. St. Hilary of Poitiers, "On Psalms 1, 53, 130," in *Selections* (Grand Rapids, MI: Eerdmans, 1955), 9:295a.
12. St. Maximus, "Sermo 105," in *Sermoni* (Alba: Edizioni Paoline, 1975), 57:740d.
13. St. Bernard, "Sermo I, 2" in *In Septuagesima,* 182:163c.
14. St. Jerome, *On Matthew,* 26:93a-c.

Chapter 2

1. St. Augustine, "Sermo 120 (De Verbis Joannis, 'In principio erat verbum')", in *Sermones* (Rome: Città Nuova, 1979) 38:677.
2. St. Cyprian, *On The Lord's Prayer,* trans. T. H. Bindley (London: 1914), 25.
3. St. John Chrysostom, *Commentary on the Gospel of St. Matthew,* 4.
4. "Second Epistle of Clement to the Corinthians, Chapter 13,

3" in *The Apostolic Fathers,* eds. Robert M. Grant and others, trans. Holt H. Graham (New York: Nelson, 1965), 124.

5. St. Augustine, "In Johannis Evangelium Tractatus CXXIV," in *Corpus Christianorum, Series Latina XXXVI* (Turnholdt, 1955), 53.

6. St. Ambrose, *De Abraham* (Rome: Città Nuova, 1984), 14:488a.

7. St. Clement of Alexandria, *Stromata, I,* (Leipzig: J. C. Hinrich, 1906), 1.

8. St. Ignatius of Antioch, "To the Philadelphians," in *Fathers of the Church,* trans. Gerald G. Walsh, S.J. (New York: Cima, 1946) 5:699c.

9. St. Jerome, "Commentarius in Ecclesiastem," III, 13, in *Corpus Christianorum, Series Latina, LXXII* (Turnholdt, 1959), 278.

10. St. Augustine, "Sermo 300 (Qualiter excipiendum sit Dei Verbum)" in *Sermones* (Rome: Città Nuova, 1979), 39:2319.

11. *Dogmatic Constitution on Divine Revelation ("Dei Verbum"),* VI, 21.

Chapter 3

1. St. Athanasius, *In Psalmum* (Columbus, OH: Hilandar Research Project, The Ohio State University, 1971), 27:487d.

2. Pope Paul VI, "Talk for Lent," 27 Feb. 1966.

3. St. Gregory the Great, *Moralium,* Book VI, 75:741a.

4. St. Ambrose, *Expositione in Psalmum* 14:114c.

5. St. Augustine, "In Johannis Evangelium, Tractatus CXXIV," in *Corpus Christianorum, Series Latina, XXXVI* (Turnholdt, 1955), 9.

6. St. Ambrose, *De Abraham* (Rome: Città Nuova, 1984), 14:488a.

7. St. John of Damascus, *De Fide Orthodoxa, Book IV,* in *A Select Library of Nicene and Post-Nicene Fathers of the Christian Church, Second Series* (Reprint, originally published by various publishers, 1898) 94:1175b.

8. St. John Chrysostom, *Homilia de Capto Eutropio et de Divitiarum Vanitate,* 52:395.

Chapter 4

1. St. Anselm, *Tractatus Asceticus,* 158:1033c.

2. Pope Paul VI, from a talk to the parishioners of St. Eusebius, Rome, 26 Feb. 1967.
3. St. Ignatius of Antioch, "Letter to the Romans," in *Fathers of the Church, I,* trans. Gerald G. Walsh, S.J. (New York: Cima, 1946), 108.
4. St. Gregory the Great, *Homiliae in Evangelium, III,* 76:1086d; quoted by Venerable Bede, *Marci Evangelium Expositio, I,* 92:166b).
5. St. Augustine, *On the Psalms,* 44, 36:508.
6. St. Clement of Alexandria, *Stromata, VII,* (Leipzig: J. C. Hinrich, 1906). 9:539c.
7. St. Gregory of Nyssa, *In Cantica Canticarum,* Homilia I; 44:778d.

PART III: THE EUCHARIST

Chapter 1

1. Thérèse of Lisieux, *Manuscrits Autobiographiques, Manuscrit "B"*. *Deuxième parte* (Lisieux, 1957) 236; Cf. *Autobiography of St. Thérèse of Lisieux,* trans. Ronald Knox (New York, 1958) 241.
2. Pierre Julien Eymard, *La Sainte Eucharistie, La Présence Réelle,* Tome I (Paris, 1949), 87.
3. Cf. *In Off. Festiv. Corp. Christi, Lecitio VI.*
4. Eymard, 142.
5. Ignatius of Antioch, *Ephesians* 19, 1 (PG 5, 660); *Ancient Christian Writers,* Vol. 1 (Westminster, Maryland, 1946), 67.
6. "Decree on the Ministry and Life of Priests," 5; *The Documents of Vatican II,* ed., Walter M. Abbott, S.J. (New York, 1966), 541.
7. J. Castellano, "Eucaristia" in *DES I* (Rome, 1975), 737.
8. *Insegnamenti di Paolo VI,* Vol. IV (Vatican, 1967), 164.
9. Pierre Benoit, cited in Castellano, 738.
10. Athanasius, *Ep. fest.* 4, 3-5 (PG 26, 1377-9).
11. Albert the Great, *De Corpore Domini* d. 1, c.2, n.7, *Opera Omnia,* ed. Auguste Borgnet (Paris, 1890-99) 38:200.
12. John Chrysostom, *In I Cor.,* hom. 24, 2 *(PG* 61, 200); cf. *The Nicene and Post-Nicene Fathers,* 1st Series, Vol. XII (Grand Rapids, 1956), 140.

Chapter 2

1. Justin, *First Apology* 1, 67, 65 *(PG* 6, 429-432, 427). *The Fathers of the Church,* Vol. 6 (New York, 1948), 106-7, 105.
2. Justin, 1, 66 (*PG* 6, 427). Translation 105 f.
3. Justin, 1, 67 (*PG* 6, 429-432). Translation 107.
4. *Didache* 9, 4. *The Fathers of the Church,* Vol. 1 (New York, 1947), 179.
5. Ignatius of Antioch. *Smyrnaeans 8* 1, (PG 5, 713 f.). *The Fathers of the church* 1:121.
6. "The Martyrdom of St. Polycarp," *The Fathers of the Church* 1:158.

7. Irenaeus, *Adv. haer.* IV, 18, 5 (*PG* 7, 1027) in *The Ante-Nicene Fathers,* (New York, 1903; American reprint of the Edinburgh edition) 1:486.

8. For this section and the two following ones, cf. Castellano, 741-745.

9. U.S. Catholic Conference, *The Order of Mass* (Washington, D.C., 1969) 88-90.

10. Paul VI, *Mysterium Fidei* (Encyclical *On Eucharist Doctrine and Worship),* no. 45 (Glen Rock, New Jersey, 1966), 44; cf. Council of Trent, *Decree On the Eucharist, chap. I.*

11. *Mysterium Fidei,* no. 27; cf. Council of Trent, *Doctrine de SS. Missae Sacrificio,* chap. 1.

12. "Constitution on the Sacred Liturgy," 47-48; *The Documents of Vatican II,* 154.

13. *Messale della Domenica* (Rome, 1973), 441-442.

Chapter 3

1. Thomas Aquinas, *Summa theologiae* III, q. 79, a. 1.

2. Thomas Aquinas, *Commentary on the Gospel of John* 6:54, 1. VII, 958.

3. Thomas Aquinas, *Comm. in I Cor.,* c. II, 1. 5.

4. Cf. Y. Congar and P. Rossano, "Proprietà Essentiale della Chiesa," *Myst. sal.* (Brescia, 1972) 469-71.

5. Cf. *The Documents of Vatican II,* 50, citing Leo the Great, *Serm.* 63, 7 (PL 54, 357).

6. Thomas Aquinas, *In Sent.* IV, D. 12, q. 2, a. 1.

7. Cyril of Jerusalem, *Cat. myst.,* 4, 3 (*PG* 33, 1100); cf. *The Fathers of the Church (Washinton, D.C., 1970) 64:181-82.*

8. Leo the Great, *Serm.* 63, 7 (*PL* 32, 357).

9. Augustine, *Confessions VII,* 10 (*PL* 32, 742), trans. F. J. Sheed (New York, 1943) 145.

10. Albert the Great, *De Euch.,* D. 3, tr. 1, c. 5 (Borgnet edition, Vol. 38, 257).

11. Albert the Great, *In IV Sent.* D. 9, a. 2 (Borgnet 29, 217).

12. Albert the Great, *De Euch.,* D. 3, tr. 1, c. 8, n. 2 (Borgnet 38, 272).

13. Thérèse of Lisieux, *Manuscrits Autobiographiques, Manuscrit "A"* 83; cf. *Autobiography of St. Thérèse of Lisieux,* trans. Ronald Knox (New York: 1958) 106.

14. A. Stoltz *Theologie der Mystik* (Regensburg, 1936), 240-1.
15. Carmel de Lisieux, "Mon ciel à moi," *Poésie de Sainte Thérèse de l'Enfant-Jésus,* (Office central de Lisieux, Lisieux, 1951) 31.
16. Carmel de Lisieux, "Le petit mendiant de noël," *Poésie de Sainte Thérse de l'Enfant-Jésus,* 105.
17. Pierre Julien Eymard, *La sainte Eucharistie, La présence réelle, Tome I* (Paris, 1949), 303-305)
18. Irenaeus, *Adv. haer.* V, 2, 3, (*PG* 7, 1124), *The Ante-Nicene Fathers,* 1:528.
19. D. van den Eynde, "L'Eucaristia in S. Ignazio, S. Giustino e S. Ireneo," in *Eucaristia* a cura di A. Piolanti (Rome 1957), 120.
20. Origen, *De orat.,* 27, 9 *(GCS* II, 365, 22-24). *Origen's Treatise on Prayer,* trans. Eric George Jay (London, 1954), 120.
21. Thomas Aquinas, *Commentary on the Gospel of John* 6:55, lect. VII, 973.
22. *Osservatore Romano,* English Edition, April 22, 1976, 1.
23. "Dogmatic Constitution on the Church," 50; *The Documents of Vatican II,* 83.
24. John of Damascus, *De fide orthodoxa* IV, 13 (*PG* 94, 1154). *The Fathers of the Church,* Vol. 37, 361.
25. P. Jacquimont, "Origen," in *L'Eucharistie chez les premiers chrétiens* (Paris, 1976), 181.
26. Albert the Great, *Super Ioannem 6, 64, Opera Omnia,* ed. Auguste Borgnet (Paris, 1890-99) 24:288.
27. Albert the Great, *De Eccl. Hierarchia* 3, 2, Opera Omnia 14:56.
28. Albert the Great, *Super 4 Sententiarium* d. 8, a. 11, *Opera Omnia* 29:206.
29. Albert the Great, *De Corpore Domini* d. 3, t. 2, c. 5, *Opera Omnia* 38:300.
30. *Insegnamenti di Paolo VI,* Vol. III (1966), 358.

Chapter 4

1. *Didache* 9, 5; 14, 1-2, *The Fathers of the Church,* 1:179-82.

2. Justin, *First Apology* 66 (*PG* 6, 427). *The Fathers of the Church,* 6:105.
3. John Chrysostom, *In Matth.,* hom. 82, 4 (*PG* 58, 743 f.). *Nicene and Post-Nicene Fathers,* first series, Vol. X, 495.
4. Origen, *In Matth. comm.,* 10, 25 (*PG* 13, 904). *The Ante-Nicene Fathers,* Origenal Supplement to the American Edition, Vol. X (New York, 1925), 431.
5. Cyprian, *De oratione dominica,* 23 *(PL* 4, 535), *The Fathers of the Church* (New York, 1958) 36:148.
6. John Chrysostom, *De prod. Judae,* 1, 6 (*PG* 49, 380-382).
7. Ignatius of Antioch, *Smyrnaeans* 9, 1 (*PG* 5, 713 f.). *The Fathers of the Church* 1:122.
8. Albert the Great, *De CorporeDomini* d. 3, t. 4, c. 3, *Opera Omnia* 38:325.
9. Thomas Aquinas, *Commentary on the Gospel of John* 6:57.
10. *Insegnamenti di Paolo VI,* (1967) 4:288.
11. Cf. *Summa theologiae* III, q. 79, a. 6, ad 3.
12. Catherine of Siena, as cited in *Il Messaggio di Santa Caterina da Siena* (Rome, 1970), 646-68.
13. Paul of the Cross, *Scritti spirituali* (Rome, 1974), 39.
14. Sacred Congregation of Rites, *Decree on the Eucharistic Mystery,* 38, in *The Pope Speaks* (1967) 12:228.
15. Cf. Castellano, 750.
16. *The Pope Speaks* (1968) 13:237.
17. E. Mersch, *The Theology of the Mystical Body,* trans. Cyril Vollert, S. J. (St. Louis and London, 1958), 592-93.
18. Cf. Cyprian, *De Oratione Dominica,* 23 *(PL* 4, 535), *The Fathers of the Church,* 36:148.
19. Cf. *Insegnamenti di Paolo VI* (1967) 4:288.
20. *Insegnamenti di Paolo VI* (1966) 3:355-59.
21. *Insegnamenti di Paolo VI* (1969) 248-49.
22. F. X. Durwell, *L'Eucharistie, présence du Christ* (Paris, 1971), 45-47.
23. Cyril of Jerusalem, *Cat. myst.* 5, 7 (*PG* 33, 1113), *The Fathers of the Church* 64:196.
24. J. Betz in *Myst. Sal.* (Brescia, 1972) 7:261-62.
25. "Decree on Ecumenism," 15; *The Documents of Vatican II,* 358.